I Need

The Ultimate Guide to Money for Teens

by POM (aka Plenty of Money)
and CF (aka Cash Flow)

I Need Money by Paul O'Mahony & Chris Farrell
www.funancialfreedom.com

Design by Luke Bunting
Research by Paul O'Mahony & Chris Farrell
© Copyright 2018 Paul O'Mahony & Chris Farrell

All rights reserved. No part of this publication may be reproduced, stored in a retrieval system, or transmitted, in any form or by any means, electronic, mechanical, photocopying, recording or otherwise, without the written permission of the authors.

Note for Librarians: A cataloguing record for this book is available from Library and Archives Canada at www.collectionscanada.gc.ca/a-z-index/index-e.html

Printed in Peterborough, Cambridgeshire,
UK ISBN: 978-1-909846-61-6

Published by Progressive Publishing
Progressive House
Units 8, 9 & 10
Cygnet Park, Forder Way, Hampton Peterborough, PE7 8GX

Website: funancialfreedom.com
Email: book@funancialfreedom.com
Twitter: @funanciallyfree
Instagram: funancialfreedom
Facebook: fb.me/funancialfreedom
Snapchat: funancial

Contents

Section 5: EARN 184

Section 6: ACCELERATE 256

Section 7: PLAY 288

Section 8: CONCLUSION 350

Acknowledgements

Firstly, thank YOU so much for picking up this book whether it is just to borrow, browse or to read.

We are so grateful for the opportunity to share with you, what we were never shown as children or as teens.

As you may know, learning how to be financially smart is not something that is emphasised in school at the moment and we hope to change that, thanks to you.

If you are a teen, YOU are the reason that we wrote this book.

We have been training adults for years on the topics of business and money, with a particular focus on internet businesses.

However, it was only after a certain thirteen-year-old named Salman came to a workshop with his Dad that the idea of this book came about'.

He was only there because the babysitter cancelled last minute, yet on the first day of the workshop, he made almost $200 in 11 minutes!

All of the adults were amazed at how quickly a teen could grasp the concepts that we were teaching compared to the grown-ups!

It came as second nature to him!

That was when we realised, we were teaching the wrong generation!

Teens understand how to use the internet and technology naturally and these are two key steps to mastering money and business!

We are so grateful to Salman and all the children and teens worldwide who inspired us to create the missing element in the educational program that we offer.

Thank you to our families, friends, colleagues and clients that have supported us on this journey!

It's time for you to learn how to become financially smart while having lots of fun and we are very grateful to you for allowing us to be your guides!

Foreword

(For old folks. Young? If so, skip this and go straight to the Introduction)

Hello parents and grandparents and anyone who has teenagers in their life.

Our aim with this book is that you will never have to hear those three words *"I Need Money"* uttered by your teen again!

Do you know the average cost to get a child from the age of 0 to 21, is $400,000?

And that's just the average!

Not only that, the total US debt for students is over one and a half trillion dollars ($1,500,000,000,000).

This means that your teenager who wants to go to college will have an average debt coming out of college of over $38,000.

Did you also know, the average person in the US has to pay $600,000 in interest on their debt over a lifetime.

Is it any wonder, that most people keep saying "*I Need Money*".

The objective of this book is to take those words "*I Need Money*" from your teens and instead have your teens start to pay you back before they're even ready for college.

This book is going to teach your children how to become financially smart and aware from a young age.

This book is going to teach your teens the importance of the basics that we never learned as children ourselves and were never shown as adults.

We strongly suggest that you also encourage your teens to check out the accompanying video content that we have created at http://funancialfreedom.com

We are thrilled that you have picked up this book, we guarantee that you will learn a lot from it, and so without further ado - lets jump in.

SECTION 1:
Introduction

CHAPTER 1:
Start Here!

"*Don't let the man bring you down.*"
– *Lawrence from School of Rock*

Welcome to *"I Need Money"* or what we really wanted to call it … "I want some freakin' money now!!"

The aim of this book is to give you, as a teen, a huge head start when it comes to one of the most important parts of your entire life…

What do you think that might be?

What ONE common topic comes up in almost every conversation you have with your friends and family, especially your parents?

What ONE thing determines how well you and your family and friends will enjoy their lives?

What is that ONE thing?

What is MY ONE thing?

Just move the letters around a little, you will find the secret…

M___Y ONE thing is MoneY!!

We bet you never noticed that before … money is all about "my one!"

We are going to show you how to become the master of all things money related!

How to earn more, have more, grow more and give more.

But before we do, who are "we"?

Our names are POM and CF aka Plenty of Money (POM) and Cash Flow (CF), and we are going to be your guides through the money journey.

It really doesn't matter how little or how much you already know on the topic, we are going to start right at the beginning and make sure no one is left behind.

Too many of us think of money as almost a mission impossible.

Too many of us think that money is something we have to "work for the man" our entire lives for.

But that is just not true!

There is a teen revolution happening right now, and you are in the perfect position to benefit.

Money is not a tricky topic; the tricky bit is we are not taught about it at school!

But you are in luck!

You don't need to plan on winning the lottery to live the life of your dreams.

In fact, we won't be leaving anything to luck in this book.

Within the pages of this book we are going to create a plan together; a clear money plan that is going to have you living a life that right now you might only be dreaming of.

We are so glad you picked up this book because we are here to show you everything you need to know about how to start making money and how to make a real difference in the world.

Are you excited?

We certainly hope so.

So, we invite you right now to keep reading for a couple more pages, and let's get started on this fantastic money journey together…

SECTION 2:
The FUN-DAMENTALS
(With an Emphasis on FUN)

CHAPTER 2:
Talk is Cheap

"The secret to getting ahead is getting started" – Mark Twain

So, a quick heads up for you.

Just having the information in this book means nothing.

You may have heard the expression 'knowledge is power.'

And you know what?

That's not true.

Knowledge itself is powerless.

Knowledge itself means nothing.

Knowledge is only the potential for power.

It only becomes power when it is applied.

The correct expression should be:

Knowledge is power when acted upon.

Knowing something is not the same as doing something with it.

The world is full of people who are very quick to shout about some knowledge they (think) they have - yet they have never done anything with it.

Maybe you've experienced this?

Has someone ever advised you about your health, yet clearly, they are not doing anything about it themselves?

Or maybe someone told you how to start a business yet they have always worked for someone else their entire life.

Or has someone told you how to make money yet they are always broke?

Be very cautious of these 'talkers'.

Talk means nothing.

Talk, as the saying goes, is cheap.

It's our ACTIONS - in other words - what we DO - that defines us.

So, you wanna be financially smart?

Well, you will need to take ACTION.

And that is what this book is all about.

Fluff-free, 'step-by-step' ACTIONABLE advice that you can start acting upon right now!

Because I'm sure, you've noticed it's easy to spend money!

A few cafe lattes here, a burrito there, a couple of songs on iTunes and a tub of hair gel, and suddenly all your money has gone.

Can you relate?

But guess what? Most people spend their entire lives like this!

Imagine NEVER being able to get out of this trap. Imagine ALWAYS having money worries.

In fact, did you know:

- Over half of American households are at risk for not having enough money to maintain their living standards.

- More than one-third of workers have less than $1,000 saved.

- Most American families are only a few missing paychecks away from insolvency.

How is this even possible in the 21st century?

I'll tell you how.

Most people are financially illiterate.

Most people are more than happy to spend money, but they do not know how to earn money.

Most people do not have financial smarts. In other words, they don't understand money.

Unlike most people - YOU clearly want to do something about it. That's awesome.

Here's the good news.

The ultimate ATM/Cash machine is the one between your ears.

Here's the bad news.

At the moment you don't know the PIN number.

Let's change that!

Want to know the secret?

The secret to getting ahead - is getting started.

Because information without execution is poverty.

So, with that in mind, let's get started.

> **TO SUM UP: The Key Takeaways from this chapter:**
> - Knowledge is only power when it is acted upon
> - The secret to getting ahead is getting started

CHAPTER 3:
Keeping it Simple

"*Happiness is the only thing worth fighting for in life.*" – *Lilly Singh*

Have you noticed, most people seem to over-complicate things?

There really is no need.

In the 13th century, there lived an English Franciscan monk called William of Ockham.

As well as being a monk, he was also a philosopher.

He was famous because of something known as Occam's razor.

This term refers to "shaving away" anything that is unnecessary to arrive at a conclusion.

For example: imagine two trees have fallen down during a windy night. Think about these two possible explanations:

Explanation 1: The wind has blown them down.

Explanation 2: A meteor crashed into them causing them to fall.

Even though both interpretations are possible, it's extremely unlikely a meteor flew into them.

Since this second explanation needs several assumptions to all to be true, it is probably the wrong answer.

Occam's razor tells us because Explanation 1 is the most straightforward answer, it is probably the right one.

At its heart, Occam's razor states that whatever is the simplest path to take, is likely to be the correct one.

This can be an extremely powerful thing to remind ourselves time and time again.

There is a skill for keeping things simple.

In fact, I'd go as far to say, that only when someone knows a subject well, can they explain it simply.

Until then, people like to over complicate things.

And so it is for making and saving and growing money.

It. Does. Not. Have. To. Be. Complicated.

There are a few simple (there's that Occam's razor) systems that you need to know to understand, make and grow money.

And we'll be sharing these systems with you in this book.

And let me tell you something else.

Systems work.

It's people that fail.

And do you know WHY most people fail?

Three main reasons: Greed, fear and impatience.

Most people want to make a lot of money, and they want it now.

Well, as you know, it doesn't work like that.

However, after educating ourselves with these few simple systems (which we are about to come onto) - making (and keeping and growing) a lot of money is something that is very possible.

So, there is no need for long and complicated drawn out systems.

Most of the time anybody that has achieved any sort of success has achieved this by keeping things simple.

Simple works.

And as you are about to discover, just having a simple system that:

A: you understand.

And

B: you implement

...is more than enough to completely change your future relationship with money.

> **TO SUM UP: The Key Takeaways from this chapter:**
>
> - The key to any sort of success, is to keep things simple.
>
> - Whatever is the simplest way to achieve something, is usually the best

CHAPTER 4:
The New Reality

"80% of success is showing up"
– Woody Allen

At the time of writing this book, the average life expectancy in America is 92.

That means it's very likely you will live to see 100 years. Imagine that - 100!

This is a far cry from just half a decade ago when the average life expectancy was 66.

People are living longer - and therefore - it stands to reason - need more money.

You may even live longer than 100 years - particularly with all the breakthroughs we are seeing in medical technology.

The body is supposedly designed to last 200 years so we'd better get saving .. LOL!

Now - whereas this is great news for you because you are young - living longer for others causes all sorts of nasty problems.

In fact - what do you think is the #1 fear of Baby Boomers? Baby Boomers, as they are known, are those people that are 65 years+.

No, it's not dying (that's their #2 fear).

It's not even illness or disease.

The #1 fear for someone over 65 years old in America -- is running out of money.

Can you believe that?

Running out of money is more scary for Baby Boomers than death.

Imagine living for 65 years and then after all that time - still having the worry of not having enough money.

Maybe you've seen this firsthand yourself - maybe from family members or family friends.

Or the countless millions of people who have to rely on (tiny) government handouts to scrape by.

True, Social Security was invented to help provide a reasonable standard of living for people aged over 65.

But it was created in 1935 when people did not live until 65, clever eh!

It was a different time then obviously.

Did you know the average monthly Social Security benefit in the US is $1,294/month.

The system wasn't designed for the world we live in today.

Here's the new reality.

The future is coming fast.

These are the facts.

- More than one-third of workers have less than $1,000 saved.

- 60% have less than $25,000 saved.

- Most scary of all - 75% of Americans can expect to see their assets disappear before they die.

In this modern world of opportunity, how can the majority of workers suffer from the very real problem that they will not have enough money to 'keep them going'?

The answer is simple. Lack of financial education.

For some reason, financial education is not taught in schools.

How to earn money is not taught in schools.

How to save money is not taught in schools.

How to grow money is not taught in schools.

How to invest money is not taught in schools.

Why is this?

One theory is that 'it's always been this way.'

Another theory is that governments don't want to pass on this information to the young at an early age - as it will allow them to realize that they CAN control their own financial destiny - and don't have to rely on a JOB.

Who knows the real reason, really all we can do is focus on ourselves.

But things are changing.

In our parent's generation, a job for life was the coveted prize.

Now, one in 2 people will be doing a different job in 2 years from now.

The new reality is these days if you want to get ahead - you have to put yourself first and get financially educated.

If you do what your parents did, you will probably be broke for life.

The world is changing and technology has changed so much that we simply must adapt or face the risk of being left behind and sadly remaining broke.

It's time to finally master money while you are still young, no matter what age that is!

Let's jump into how to make, save, invest and grow your money.

See you in the next Chapter!

TO SUM UP: The Key Takeaways from this chapter:

- The average life expectancy these days is 92 in the USA

- You could very easily live to way beyond 100.

- The #1 fear for most adults in America is running out of money.

CHAPTER 5:
Secret of the Rich

"The best investment you can make is in yourself" – Warren Buffett

I really encourage you not to skip the next few pages -- but to read slowly and surely and digest every word here.

Because if you really take on board what you are about to discover and implement it - you will become financially successful for the rest of your life.

A grand claim indeed - so let me explain.

Above all else - wealthy people are not wealthy because of some complex strategy.

They are wealthy because they are prepared to apply principles that other people are not willing to apply.

To put it simply - wealthy people do things that other people are not prepared to do.

So, let me ask you a question.

Are you willing to do things that 99% of others are not prepared to?

Here is an interesting fact for you!

0.24% of the entire population of the planet are millionaires!

So, if you do what 99.8% of people do with money, you will never join the millionaire club!

Here's the good news, 99% of people will never read this book or implement the learnings, but you will!

Most of your friends will not be prepared to do what it takes.

Most of your friends will want to hang out at the Mall or play the latest version of GTA.

But guess what?

Most of your friends will never be rich.

That doesn't make them bad people, it just makes them people who will struggle around money for life.

How about you?

Are you prepared to do what it takes to change your financial future?

Are you sure?

Let's see.... ☺

One habit that the rich honor - is TIME.

The rich understand that time is more important than money.

You can lose a dollar and make it back.

But you lose an hour, or a day, or a month - you can't make that back.

So, how do the rich honor their time?

By spending it wisely in EDUCATION.

This book is all about teaching you to be financially smart.

And it starts with EDUCATION.

Let me tell you a secret.

The quickest way to learn anything is to find someone who has achieved what it is you want, and to copy them.

Copy them from afar.

Or ask them for help, ask them to teach you.

You'll be amazed at how many people are happy to help, if only you ask.

You can only go so far trying to do things on your own.

If you want to speed up any level of success in your life - you need to learn from someone who achieved your goal.

These people are known as coaches or mentors.

Even professional athletes that make millions of dollars every year have mentors.

Because mentors have been there, they've been battle-hardened in the trenches, and come out the other side.

Mentors bring a perspective that allows us to see the bigger game.

So, why are we mentioning this?

Well, let's go straight to the top.

If we want to learn how to become financially smart, let's not waste time with the small fish, let's go straight to the top guys.

How about the richest man in the world? Imagine having him as a mentor.

In fact, the wealthiest man in the world often changes between a few individuals, but one guy who has always been in this list for the last 30 years, is Warren Buffett.

You may have heard of him.

Warren Buffett is universally loved for not only his incredible business success (and it's worth noting he made all his money, he wasn't born into it) - but he's also loved for how much he gives away to charities and foundations, and the amount of good his wealth has helped bring to others.

But first and foremost, he is a businessman.

In an interview given for his authorized biography The Snowball, Buffett was asked what his advice was to become financially smart.

Ready for his answer?

He said: "I just sit in my office and learn."

This could be summed up in one word:

EDUCATION.

Warren Buffett has committed to lifelong learning.

He LEARNS something every day.

In fact, he goes on to say that he likes to go to bed smarter than when he woke up.

And he's the wealthiest man in the world.

Maybe he's onto something.

Everything STARTS with education.

Becoming a little wiser every day.

Would you be down for this?

Not everybody is.

In fact, 99.8% of people are not.

Most people would rather check Instagram, read some online news, and scroll through their News Feed, rather than continually educate themselves.

However, most people are not worth almost $100 billion (which is almost how much Warren Buffett is worth)

Look, I get it. Short term, checking Insta and Twitter is fun.

But long term, the investment you make in educating and improving yourself will go so much further.

And that's the secret to becoming rich: you have to commit to investing in yourself.

Let me repeat: you have to commit to investing in yourself.

You have to cultivate curiosity.

You have to strive to become a little wiser every day.

Essentially - if I had to sum it all up - if you want to get rich - you have to decide right here and now to invest some TIME to LEARN.

So, let me ask you.

Are you?

Because let me tell you something.

If you're not willing to LEARN, no one can help you.

However, if you are prepared to learn, no one can stop you.

You MUST LEARN for the right to EARN!

So why isn't everyone wealthy?

Simple. Because as we've discussed, most people don't want to educate themselves.

But why is this, if we know that educating ourselves results directly in financial success?

Let me tell you.

Mark Twain once said, "I never let my schooling get in the way of my education."

What he meant by this is, we often get confused between school and education.

Most people don't love school - and so by default - most people feel the same about education.

If we hate school, we will be opposed to education from a young age.

So, we need to remove this mental barrier that many have when it comes to education.

Learning is cool.

Learning is sexy.

Learning is the foundation that's going to allow you to get what you want, to look after your family, to help get that girl or guy that you want, and create the life of your dreams.

However, most people would rather scroll through their phone than learn some new skills.

Here's the good news, you can scroll through your phone and ALSO learn the skills that you need.   And we will speak more about this later.

But if you are open to educating yourself with some financial skills, then you are going to become unstoppable.

And there's more good news.

Think about any skills that you may already have.

Maybe you can play a musical instrument, or speak a different language. Perhaps you can rap, or you can code, perhaps you're good at a particular sport, or maybe you're good at writing.

Whatever skills you have, the one thing that all skills have in common is that they are learnable.

Think about it - every skill that you have - you have learned.

And making money - is a skill.

So, therefore - just like ANY skill - it can be learned.

Pumped? You should be.

Ready to learn? Good. Let's go.

SUM UP:

- The Secret to becoming Rich is to have good habits
- The most important habit is to spend time every day LEARNING
- Making money is a skill, and just like ANY skill, it can be LEARNED

CHAPTER 6:
The Importance of Being Specific

"The more of wisdom we know, the more we may earn." – *The Richest Man in Babylon*

Here's one thing about generating income.

There is a truth and a reality in life.

Money has rules.

And they are as real as gravity. And people that have money understand these rules.

Financial literacy is one of the greatest gifts you can bestow upon yourself.

But guess what? It will come as no surprise to you that less than 1% of the population is financially smart.

Sure - 100% want to enjoy the rewards of wealth - but less than 1% know the rules to get there.

Are you beginning to see the problem?

I could sum up the #1 rule to being financially smart as follows;

To make money - you need to have your own SYSTEM.

So - ask yourself - do you have a system?

Probably not - and that's ok - as we are going to teach you.

But do most people have a system? Short answer, no.

And I'm not talking about a JOB.

Because a JOB is not a system.

A JOB makes your boss or the company rich, not you.

The Average American saves less than $2000 year. So, a JOB is not the answer.

No - you need your OWN system.

Not only that - but a simple system that is easy to understand and implement.

Human beings are fundamentally like a herd of animals, have you noticed? Sometimes they are known as sheeple!

So, if you don't have your OWN system - there is a 100% chance that you will become part of someone else's system - spending your time - your ideas - your efforts - for somebody else.

And guess what.

You are never going to become rich while in somebody else's system.

Most people would probably say they do have a goal to do better financially in the next 12 months.

But that's vague and generic.

Our question to them would be - if you are serious about making more money in the next 12 months - what is your SYSTEM to achieve this?

Tell me EXACTLY what you are going to do. And I mean EXACTLY. What's Step 1 in your system? Let alone steps 2 and 3...?

Most people don't know.

So, let's change that.

One thing that is very important when it comes to achieving anything is to be SPECIFIC.

Specific Information is better than generic.

For any system to work, it needs to be specific.

Most people have vague plans in life.

And when it comes to the subject of wealth, most people have general aims.

Most people will say something like 'I want to be rich'.

And then they will wonder why they don't have the things they really want.

Most of the time it's because they didn't take any SPECIFIC steps to get there.

School is very good for getting a solid education but mostly it gives you generic intelligence.

But it is only when we seek specific knowledge, that success will follow.

So, with that in mind, lets jump into a SPECIFIC plan that is going to make you financially smart.

TO SUM UP: The Key Takeaways from this chapter:

- Specific information is better than generic
- To make money you need to follow a proven system

SECTION 3:
Leaping Ahead of the Rest

CHAPTER 7:
L.E.A.P.

"Leap, and the net will appear"
– John Burroughs

So, now we know we want to keep things simple.

We also know the importance of education and having a specific plan to follow.

Feels good, right?

Now it's time to put some meat on the bones.

Here at *I Need Money*, we want to introduce you to something we call LEAP.

LEAP is a process that we are about to teach you that will allow you to become financially smart.

Now we totally understand you may already have fears and questions popping up in your head like burned toast.

For now - all we ask is you are open to what we are about to share with you.

In other words - we want you to open your heart and open your mind and surrender to the process.

Trust that we have your back here.

Trust that what we have for you - is not only simple - but arguably more important - it is ENJOYABLE.

Let me share something with you, it's so much easier to make money when you enjoy what you are doing.

So, trust in the Process.

The LEAP process.

SO - what exactly is this LEAP thing we've just mentioned?

Well, the rest of this book is dedicated to the LEAP process, and it works as follows.

There are 4 steps to **LEAP**.

The **L** stands for **LEARN**.

The **E** stands for **EARN**.

The **A** stands for **ACCELERATE**.

The **P** stands for **PLAY**.

Each of these 4 components is integral to your success (and enjoyment) of making money.

So, let's look at them in a bit more detail.

LEARN.

As we have already discussed - anyone who is financially successful has taken the time to EDUCATE themselves first.

This is the all-important first step.

Remember, the secret to becoming rich that we shared with you in Chapter 3. DO you remember what it was?

Let me remind you.

The secret to becoming rich was: you have to commit to investing in yourself.

And how do we do this?

Simple.

By learning.

This is where everything STARTS.

Making money is the end destination. But we can't start at the end. We need to know how to get there. We need to understand the journey that lays ahead.

And this is your roadmap.

It starts with LEARNING.

What that means is - we are going to teach you some core fundamentals to financial wealth. With the emphasis on FUN!

In the LEARN step, we will share with you how money works.

We are about to educate you, so you really understand how saving works and how investing works.

These are skills that once learned will stay with you for your entire life.

And as you are about to discover, it does not have to be complicated.

In LEARN you will discover that educating yourself on a subject that can directly impact your life and the life of your family, is one of the most addictive and satisfying things you can do.

You wait, you will be EXCITED to learn — as you will realize that your LEARNING is directly correlated to you MAKING MONEY.

LEARN is where we focus on getting you up to speed and EDUCATED.

So - that's LEARN!

After LEARN — we jump into step 2 of LEAP - the E.

And the E stands for EARN.

Now that we have educated ourselves with a handful of financial skills from the LEARN step - in EARN, we will implement some of what we have just learned.

This is where things are going to get REALLY exciting!

Because in EARN we are going to share with you SPECIFIC (there's that word again!) actionable steps that you can take RIGHT NOW - to start making money.

We will do this by sharing with you in the EARN step — 37 business ideas that you can set up from home - that can all make you money.

In EARN we will share with you exactly how to set these businesses up.

Do you remember back in Chapter 1 we talked about keeping things simple?

There is a reason we wanted to start this book with that.

Because as we discussed back then, most people seem to over-complicate things.

And as we said, there really is no need.

The reason we wanted to flag that up again here - is because the same will be applied when it comes to creating a business for you.

Prepare to have your eyes well and truly opened as to what you can achieve.

The business ideas we will be sharing with you will be a mixture of traditional "offline" businesses that you don't need a computer for - as well as "online" businesses that you could run from a smartphone!

Now - one quick thing - please don't worry or start to say to yourself 'but I don't know the first thing about creating a business.'

That's totally ok.

As we have said a few times now, we want you to trust us and surrender to this process.

There is a SYSTEM here.

Success leaves clues.

Anyone that has been successful has followed a set of guidelines to get something done.

And this LEAP process is designed to show you step by step the guidelines for you to take.

So, whereas we understand the thought of creating a business may be scary, as you are about to discover, when you are taken by the hand and shown step by step how to achieve this, the reality is it's a lot simpler than you think.

And in the EARN step, you will discover this for yourself!

So, step 1 is to LEARN. Step 2 is EARN.

Then we move onto Step 3 which is ACCELERATE.

In ACCELERATE - once we have educated you about money, and once we have started to earn some money, in this third step, we will show you how to GROW your money.

This will be achieved through investing wisely, saving smartly, and delaying gratification.

In Accelerate we will share with you exact tricks, tips and techniques to turn your money into something that works for you and not the other way around.

You may have heard of the saying 'money makes money' and it's absolutely correct.

But it's only valid if you know the rules and you know what you are doing.

And we will share these rules with you in ACCELERATE.

And that brings us onto the final step in LEAP. The P.

PLAY!!

I'm sure you have many ideas of what you would like to use your money for, but there are also things that you can do with your money that I bet you have not thought about.

Think of the good you can do.

Think of those you could help.

Think of the impact you can make.

Let me share something with you — most people think all they want to do is make money.

And while that is great - when people make a lot of money something interesting happens.

After a while, they realize there is more to life than just making money.

You may not think that right now as you read this, but there is.

There is something greater.

The next level is legacy.

Sure - it would be great to be financially independent and look after your family - but the more money you make - the more you will begin to feel that there is 'something more.'

This is where legacy comes in.

Giving back.

Inspiring others.

Passing on your knowledge.

Supporting others less fortunate than you.

In PLAY - as well as sharing with you some fun ideas that you may not have even thought about - we will also share with you how your new found money making skills can be used make a real impact in the lives of others.

Ironically that is something you can't put a price on, but the satisfaction you will get will be priceless.

You may not realize it as you read this - but your legacy will reward and satisfy you in ways that you can't fathom right now.

So - that's LEAP!

Learn. Earn. Accelerate. Play.

That's the process of how to make and grow money.

So - now we know the theory - let's go and actually do it.

Now - just before we jump in and get started - let me ask you a question.

How are you feeling?

Be honest.

How do you feel right now?

Of course, the prospect of being rich is exciting, but also at the same time, now that you understand there is a PROCESS to achieve this - and that starts with you LEARNING - it is understandable if you feel a bit nervous.

In fact - many people at this point suddenly get a bit scared.

Because now it's becoming a reality.

As you read these words, you are at a crossroads in your life.

We are about to travel down a new path.

We are about to learn some new skills.

And anything new can be scary.

So, lets quickly talk about this.

If you are feeling a bit scared or daunted at the path ahead, let's talk about your relationship with FEAR.

TO SUM UP: The Key Takeaways from this chapter:

- Everything starts with EDUCATION

- In this book we will be sharing with you the LEAP process. This is the fastest way to become financially smart.

- LEAP stands for LEARN - EARN - ACCELERATE - PLAY

CHAPTER 8:
The Rule of FEAR

Let me tell you how to ruin your life.

You ruin your life by letting your past govern it.

You ruin your life when you compare yourself to others.

It has been proven time after time, that the way we look at our life is essentially a barometer of our expectations.

This is based on what we've been taught we are worthy of having and capable of achieving.

These influences are mostly inspired by external forces – such as family, upbringing, and community.

How do you view the business of making money? Be honest.

Do you believe that you will have to learn a few things first, but it can be done?

Or secretly deep down inside do you think you can't do it.

If you choose the first answer - that's great.

But even if you choose the second — you need to be congratulated on being honest with yourself.

Let me tell you this clearly and plainly.

Making money IS something that you can achieve - but the FIRST step – is to address how you find yourself thinking about this subject matter.

Are you plagued by negative thoughts?

The 'yeahs' – the ' buts'?

If so, it is critical that you cut those thoughts off as soon as they start.

You need to hit the delete button every time doubt appears.

Easier said than done though right?

Fear can make your business drown!

Of course, we all suffer from it.

But it's how we react to fear – not fear itself - that makes the difference between success and failure.

We are ALL scared! Get over it!

Can I let you into a deep dark secret that festers away in most people but is rarely spoken about?

Most people secretly like fear.

Why?

Because fear is a very handy and convenient excuse that we can use when we are not really doing what we want with our lives.

How many times have we heard or have we said to ourselves 'I can't do that – I'm not good enough – I'm not talented enough - I don't have time – It's not for me – I'm not good looking enough- I'm too old – I'm too young...'

Fear can be a very useful tool that many use to convince themselves that NOT taking action is indeed the correct path – because 'somebody else could do it but not me...'

It's NOT the fears themselves you should be concerned about – it's how you REACT and RESPOND to them that will determine if you succeed or fail.

Do you see the difference? A lot of people don't.

When fear raises its head - it presents us with a choice.

Do I give up because of this fear – or do I push through despite this fear?

Check out what this guy did. You may have heard of him:

In 1928, when Walt Disney was only 26 years old, he drew a cartoon of a mouse.

Walt was convinced that this drawing of a mouse would do very well in a new style of movies that was beginning to emerge, called animation.

However - he needed about $20,000 to make this happen.

In today's money - that is over $1million.

Walt decided to visit as many banks as it would take, to hopefully find a bank manager who shared his vision.

How many banks do you think Walt visited?

Five? Ten? Twenty?

Walt visited over 302 banks before he found one prepared to take a chance with him.

302!

Would you have done the same?

It has been proven that successful people can hit delete to fear – as they have a clear and defined vision of what the end result is.

Here are some more famous and not-so-famous real-life examples of individuals who hit the delete button to fear on their path to success.

- 'Nobody will watch a show about nothing...' – what Jerry Seinfeld and co-creator Larry David were first told when they began to pitch Seinfeld.

- "No, thank you, we're not interested...' - what Brian Acton was told in 2009 when he applied for a job at Facebook. As a result, Brian went off a co-founded WhatsApp, which he ended up selling to Facebook 5 years later, for $19 billion. Yes, billion!

- 'There's no market for it. If there were, major airlines would already be offering it...' – conclusion given to Fred Smith, founder of FedEx.

- 'Nobody will use the mail to rent movies' - what Blockbuster said to Netflix. Interesting to note which one is still around

- 'A global, twenty-four-hour news network will never work...' – network executives' response to Ted Turner's plans for CNN.

- 'We Don't Like Their Sound. Groups of Guitars Are On Their Way Out" - a record executive at Decca comments to The Beatles as he turned them down

Here are two things you need to remember when it comes to FEAR.

1.   Fear is A FALSE EXPECTATION APPEARING REAL.

Most of our fears are imaginary and mainly based on worrying about things that may never happen.

2.   Fear is worrying about what other people think.

This fear cripples people!

Perhaps you thought about asking someone to the prom, and you were too afraid, not because of the fear of rejection, but just as much as what your friends would say when they heard about the rejection!

So much of what we do and don't do, especially as teens, is because we worry about what others think of us!

But 99% of those people will be broke so does it really matter?

Say this with me ... "What other people think of me is NONE of my business."

Sing it, shout it, print it out and stick it on every mirror in your house.

One more time "What other people think of me is NONE of my business."

You are now officially ready to make the LEAP!

TO SUM UP: The Key Takeaways from this chapter:

- Fear is always going to be in your life to some degree, and that's ok

- The secret is managing how we react and respond to it

- When we feel scared we are presented with a choice. Do I give up because of this fear – or do I push through despite this fear?

SECTION 4: LEARN

CHAPTER 9:
LEARN - Introduction

"You conquer fear through knowledge." – anon

Confucius, the Chinese teacher and philosopher, famously said 'a journey of a thousand miles starts with a single step.'

Are you ready for your first step?

So now we understand, that this all-important first step - is all about EDUCATING yourself.

And that's what this section - LEARN - is all about.

Here in LEARN, we are going to get SMART about money.

And we are going to do this together.

We are about to get you on the path to understanding all you need to know about money, from earning - to saving - to investing - to growing - to sharing.

And what better place to start than at the very beginning...

The History Of Money

CHAPTER 10:
The History of Money

"*An investment in knowledge pays the best interest.*" – Benjamin Franklin

Have you ever wondered how money came to be....?

Let's take a little journey for a moment ....

A journey back in time, tens of thousands of years ago, when we have cavemen and cavewomen, cave boys and cave girls.

Imagine this for a moment, MONEY does not exist!

There are no dollars or euros.... no credit or debit cards and no banks or bank accounts.... and no shops!

How did people even survive you might wonder???

The concept seems so foreign to us that it really can be challenging to wrap our heads around this BUT this was how life was at one point in time!

So ... how did things work?

Well, to begin with, we were self-sufficient. What does this mean?

Well, it means that our ancestors had the same basic needs as we do today, like food and drink, clothing and shelter etc., but instead of buying these with money (which didn't exist), they went out and acquired each item by themselves.

They hunted for food or picked it from trees, they milked cows, they used the hides of animals for clothing and they built homes from trees or moved into caves.

However, over time, peoples' skills became more specialized.

For example, some people decided to focus on herding cattle, while others concentrated on making clothing and others focused on building shelters and homes.

People started to focus on doing the things they preferred rather than doing everything!

Eventually, a system of "bartering" was introduced so that people could swap one service for another.

For example, a farmer who cared for cows could exchange things like milk and cheese with someone who cared for sheep so they could receive the wool for warm clothing.

Over time as you might imagine, it became difficult to know the exact worth each item had.

How much milk was enough to exchange for some meat for example?

The word "capital" which is often used nowadays as another word for money comes from the word "kaput" meaning the head of a cow!

What began to happen was certain items were used that were easier to exchange, and became a "currency" rather than directly swapping products.

Items such as feathers, precious stones, metals like gold and copper, jewellery, salt and even flowers were used as "types" of money.

Over time, approximately 3,000 years ago, these became coins and then more recently, they became paper notes.

Over the past thirty years, plastic cards took the place of paper, and in today's world, money can be exchanged online without anything physical being exchanged at all!

Money can now move at the speed of light!

You can transfer money to a friend on the other side of the world in a millisecond.

In essence, money is nothing more than a means of exchange.

Today, a brand new means for exchanging money called cryptocurrencies like bitcoin has arrived, and this is an entirely new way to manage money.

At present, the central banks control the amount of "real" money that exists in different countries.

With cryptocurrencies, the banks become less involved in the process.

We will discuss cryptocurrencies in much more detail as we move through the training.

So, that's a whistle-stop tour as to how money even came to exist.

Let's carry on with LEARN - and in the next chapter - we want to share with you the '5 Levels of Wealth'.

Which one are you? Which one does your family belong to?

Let's find out....

TO SUM UP: The Key Takeaways from this chapter:

- Whereas the types of money have changed over the years (from cattle to coins) the one thing that has remained constant is that money is simply a means of exchange.

CHAPTER 11:
The 5 Levels of Wealth

"Opportunity is missed by most people because it is dressed in overalls and looks like work" – *Thomas Edison*

In this chapter, let's explore the 5 Levels of Wealth.

Get this.

Recent studies carried out on people that are 65 years old in the USA show that only 1% are considered rich, 4% are deemed comfortable financially, 5% are still working in a job, 56% need financial support from the government or their families and 34% are dead.

In other words, at 65 years of age, 95% of people are either dead or dead broke!

We don't want you to be in the same situation!

These statistics are truly frightening and show why it is so important for us to get our finances in order from a young age.

This is why you are so smart to start learning how to completely change things for you and your family starting today!

So, with that in mind, let's identify the universal 5 levels of wealth that exist.

1. Debt

People can be divided into five different areas based on their relationship with money.

The first of these is DEBT.

Debt is a scary word, but it is something that is hugely important to understand and has an impact on almost everybody in the world.

Debt describes when you are worth less than zero.

Now - please understand this...

Most people on the planet are in debt.

Most people on the planet are living day by day in debt, trying to get to above zero.

But what exactly does this mean?

Your debt is the amount of money that you have borrowed to live on.

If you have taken out a loan, this is what is known as debt.

For example, when you purchase a house, this house loan is a debt (as I'm sure you know it's called a mortgage).

Interestingly, the word "mortgage" comes from the word "mortir" meaning death!

In other words, getting a mortgage means debt until death!!!

It probably shouldn't come as a surprise to you to discover that the number one reason for death is heart disease which is caused primarily by stress.

The number one reason for divorce too is due to fighting over money.

Why?

Because when people are in debt and when money is scarce, people become very stressed and emotional about it.

Here's something important to realize: It's very easy to get into debt very quickly.

Debt is often used as a quick fix to get out of a problem when you would do anything just to get some money now and then worry about paying it back later.

However, this is the habit that can lead to living in debt for an entire lifetime.

The good news is through learning some financial smarts you can get out of debt and climb the ladder of the 5 levels of wealth.

Also - it is worth mentioning - that there is something known as Good Debt. We'll come onto Good Debt later in this chapter.

2. Scarcity

The next level above Debt — is scarcity.

Back in 2008 and 2009, which is a long time ago now, over 450,000 Americans completed a study around money.

The study was carried out by a very well known Nobel prize-winning economist, Daniel Kahneman.

He found that when people earned less than $75,000, they were stuck in the scarcity zone.

Think about this for a moment.

Now, this was over a decade ago, so if we factor in inflation (which is about 1.6% on average per year) $75,000 back then would be worth approximately $90,000 now.

According to this study, anyone who earns $90,000 or less is in this 'scarcity zone'.

This means that every decision you make on a daily basis is determined by how much money you have access to.

As a teenager, you will know exactly how this feels!!

You can't do what you want to do, because you simply don't have the money to do it!

But imagine how this would feel for your entire life...

Of course, this is not what we want!

Think about this though.

Living in the Scarcity Mindset means that when you eat in a restaurant, what you want to eat is first determined by the prices on the menu.

In fact, let me ask you a question.

Do you know anyone who looks at the prices on a menu before they look at the choice of food?

If you do - then they are living in a scarcity mindset.

Another example is choosing where to go on vacation. If the price is the determining factor, then you are living in the scarcity mindset.

I'm sure you recognize people that think like this because here's the thing, most people do.

In fact, most people on the planet are either in the Debt or the Scarcity zone — and this is how they live their lives.

Debt and Scarcity are seen as 'normal'.

Let's make a promise: don't be normal! Ok? Good ☺

As a slight aside - many of these people in Debt or Scarcity will tell you that money isn't that important.

But the truth is lack of money impacts their lives more than it does with people who have lots of money.

Another interesting fact is that most adults that are stuck in Debt or in the Scarcity Zone continue to act in the same way and do the same things that got them into the situation in the first place.

Most people find debt and scarcity so overwhelming that they just block it out and hope it will just 'magically' go away.

Unfortunately, it very rarely does.

Something dramatic has to change to get to the next level.

Warren Buffett famously says that the "Chains of habit are too light to be felt until they are too heavy to be broken."

Isn't that a powerful quote?!

It means that the longer you leave this problem without addressing it, the more likely it is that you will never get out of it.

Just ask graduate students in the US, and they will know what this means!

Starting out in the real world owing $38,000 on average before they even have a house or a family!

We can change this outcome from a very young age by getting focused on three key things.

First, comes getting educated in the right areas of your life.

And this is what we are covering here in this LEARN section. And as you know by now - the more you learn, the more you can earn!

Secondly, we need to have a specific system that we can follow that will allow us to make money. That's what we will be covering in the EARN section.

And then the third step is to learn how to make that money work for you and how you can use your time and money in a way that allows you to become even wealthier by working fewer hours.

This is what we cover in ACCELERATE, where we will show you how to transform your money and time into creating amazing wealth.

3. Healthy

So let's continue to climb the ladder of the 5 levels of Wealth.

The next level is known as Healthy.

This does not mean physical health (although interestingly for most people there is a correlation between being financially healthy and physically healthy)

Regarding your wealth - Healthy does not necessarily mean that you are rich, but it does mean you are getting there.

You have a clear plan in place to become financially free, just like you will very soon.

You have more than enough money to cover your bills and still, have some left over, and you are feeling good about your financial health.

There are no studies that share exactly how much money you need to be earning to be in the "Health" zone, but a fair ballpark figure would be $100,000 year.

If someone is making this per annum, expect them to be in the Healthy Zone.

As a teenager, it is very doable to get you into this zone very quickly as you should not have amassed any debt at this point (or at least very little) but your earning potential or your ability to earn an income is HUGE!

In fact, I suspect you may now even be aware of your potential right now!

And that's fine.

But the more you continue to flex and grow your financial muscles as you are doing right now, the more of an advantageous situation you are going to find yourself in very soon.

You might find it interesting to know that as an adult, it is much more difficult to get to the healthy zone.

This is mainly because most adults have lots of habits that make it very difficult to get out of debt or scarcity.

It's also worth mentioning that where things go wrong for teenagers, is when they take on student debt.

Student debt can take 20 years (or more) to recover from!

20 years!

It just doesn't make any sense to go into debt for this long — so why do a lot of people?

The simple answer is a lot of people get pressurized by people around them to do it because it is "normal".

BUT "normal" means being in the debt or scarcity zones and they are the last places we want to be!

We want to be in the next two zones.

4. Prosperity

The next zone is the Prosperity Zone.

In the prosperity zone, we are truly starting to get ahead.

Covering the bills is not the goal any more, that has been taken care of a long time ago.

We are now in the business of business.

We are helping people on a significant scale and getting rewarded for it handsomely.

We have multiple sources of income meaning that we no longer have to rely on a single job that we could potentially lose at any time.

Not only do we have lots of sources of money but we also have our money making us more money.

We have automated savings plans and lots if investment strategies in place.

We are helping other businesses out by investing in them early which helps us make even more money.

We are able to make decisions without ever having to think about the cost of how much will it be.

We are financially free and never need to work a day in our lives again if we do not wish.

Our interest on our investments alone is enough for us to live off which is what we cover in ACCELERATE.

Which brings us on to the 5th level in the 5 Levels of Wealth.

The very top level is:

5. Wealthy

This is where you'll find people that always have excess cash. They have everything they want in life. If they don't, they know how to get it.

They do not think in scarcity.

They have abundant cash flow systems in place.

But they also are wise enough to realize that they still need to LEARN continually.

The wealthy understand that the way to success is through the continuous pursuit of knowledge.

The wealthy are life long learners.

They are generous and successful, and people gravitate towards them, hoping that some of their success will rub off on them.

The wealthy have systems that allow them to earn, spend, save, invest, and give away their money in the wisest ways possible.

The wealthy also understand that when challenges come their way - as they will for everybody — these challenges are in fact opportunities.

The wealthy understand that challenges are not sent to destroy us, but instead as an opportunity to promote, increase and strengthen us.

The wealthy are not fazed by challenges, whereas those in Debt and Scarcity are often destroyed by them.

The wealthy take responsibility for what is happening in their life.

Those in Debt and Scarcity blame other people/things.

So — which of the 5 levels do you want to inhabit?

I think we all know the answer to that ☺

Reaching wealthy is very achievable if you really want to change and are closely following what we are sharing with you.

As we have said a thousand times, everything starts with LEARNING, so well done for investing your time in LEARNING these financial smarts.

We've already covered how money came to be, and now the 5 Levels of Wealth.

Let's continue with our LEARNING - and let's move onto another important thing that you need to understand. The power of Saving.

TO SUM UP: The Key Takeaways from this chapter:

- There are 5 levels of Wealth
- Debt - Scarcity - Healthy - Prosperity - Wealthy
- Everybody will fit into one of these levels

CHAPTER 12:
Savings

"You must learn to save first and spend afterwards." – John Poole

In the last chapter we looked at the 5 levels of wealth, and we highlighted the alarming fact that the majority of the people on the planet live in debt and scarcity.

In fact, it's highly likely that members of your own family are in this situation, so you have probably experienced this first hand yourself.

However, it's important that you realize that to break out of debt and scarcity requires more than just the ability to earn money.

It also requires the ability to save money.

The rich understand that SAVING is the foundation of wealth.

Saving money, of course, means merely setting money aside to spend in the future.

But saving - done correctly — can earn you more money than you ever thought possible!!

Anyone that has made a lot of money will say the same thing: the first step to turning your money into riches is to learn the basics of saving.

This is one of the secrets of the rich.

Becoming wealthy means learning how to save.

Let me repeat!

Becoming wealthy means learning how to save.

In 1926 a book called 'The Richest Man in Babylon' was published.

One hundred years on, this book is still regarded as the 'bible' for financial growth and money management.

That, of course, will be now replaced by this book ... LOL

And guess what?

What do you think a lot of the book focuses on?

You got it! Saving!

Here is a powerful section taken from the book that shows the importance of saving.

"Wealth, like a tree, grows from a tiny seed. The first coin you save is the seed from which your tree of wealth shall grow. The sooner you plant that seed, the sooner shall the tree grow. And the more faithfully you nourish and water that tree with consistent savings, the sooner may you bask in contentment beneath its shade."

Powerful, huh?

Now here's something crazy.

Saving sounds simple, doesn't it?   But remember that over half of the adult population in the US have less than $1,000 worth of savings.

Over half!! Less than $1,000 saved! Insane (and scary).

That's because people are good spenders - but bad savers.

Spending money sounds exciting, whereas saving money sounds boring.

But let me tell you, everyone who is rich, has learned to be a good saver.

So, let me repeat one more time as I want you to remember this!

One of the secrets of the wealthy is learning how to save.

And the good news is - as we continue through this book - we are going to turn you into a great saver.

Saving is absolutely essential for you to have any chance of becoming rich.

If someone is not saving money, by default they are probably spending it, which means they need to go back again to make more — and they get stuck in this endless, exhausting cycle that often lasts for their entire life.

This is known as the RAT RACE.

And I'm sure you've heard of it.

The RAT RACE means that someone works hard for their money, but doesn't save anything, and so continually keeps repeating the process, often forever.

The RAT RACE is why most of the world are in debt or in scarcity. They don't know how to SAVE.

Let me repeat!

Most people DO NOT KNOW HOW TO SAVE!

Did you know that one in four American adults do not have a SINGLE penny saved.

One in four!

So, the headline is - we MUST save!

Got it?

And don't underestimate saving a little here and a little there. Small savings add up.

For example, most supermarkets have a Customer Loyalty Card that allows users to save on purchases.

Imagine you saved just $11 a week using this card. At the end of the year, you would have saved $572. That's a lot of money that I'm sure you could find a use for....!

It is never too early (or too late) to start saving.

By putting savings in a bank or investing it (which we will come onto), you can let your money work for you.

This is also known as the power of compounding (which we will also come onto).

So - now we know that we must save - the big question, of course, is HOW do we do this effectively? Even if you have next to nothing to start with?

Well - the dollar amount that you save does not matter - what DOES matter - is that we need to make saving a HABIT.

And you may like to know that we are going to make this really easy for you.

We have a system that you can start to use straight away that will set you up with some fantastic habits to set you on the path to riches!

In fact - we want to break this system down for you STEP BY STEP as it is that important. And we will do this in the ACCELERATE section here in this book.

So, please know that we will come back to HOW to save effectively later in this book.

For now - just be aware that saving is a skill you will need to get good at (and we will make sure you will!)

TO SUM UP: The Key Takeaways from this chapter:

- The rich understand that SAVING is the foundation to wealth

- Becoming wealthy means learning how to save.

- The reason why most people live in debt or scarcity is that they don't know how to SAVE

CHAPTER 13:
Needs & Wants

"Wealth consists not in having great possessions, but in having few wants" – *Epictetus*

Let's talk about needs and wants!

Because the relationship between the two is an important concept to understand.

Needs are things we must have to survive.

Wants, on the other hand, are things that we'd like to have, but that aren't necessary for survival.

Here's the Golden Rule: Basic money management is taking care of needs first, wants second.

There are obvious things that we need: Food, water, shoes, clothes, school books, pens, etc.

And then there are lots of things that we want: Concert tickets, a new phone, contact lenses, a puppy.

The confusion can arise when we are not sure if something is a need or a want.

For example, is a pair of sneakers a need or a want?

Well, one pair would be a need. However, if you desired a few pairs of dope kicks just because you liked them, then that would be a want.

The challenge is being strict with ourselves — because advertisers are out to get us!

I'm not kidding.

We live in a world where the pressure to spend money is constant.

You are surrounded by ads all the time.

From websites to messaging apps to YouTube to bus sides, from magazines to Amazon to your favorite online influencers and Instagram Stories: advertisers are even placing product placement in movies and TV shows and in your favorite video games.

Your favorite celebrity is paid to wear a particular brand in the hope that you will buy something to be like them.

Every sports team is sponsored with a hope that you may use the brand emblazoned across their chest.

In fact, did you know we are bombarded with over 10,000 advertisements a day.

All with ONE objective - to get our money!

So, that's why it pays (no pun intended) to be a master at filtering between a need and a want.

Of course, there is nothing wrong with buying a few wants now and again.

However - remember what we discussed in the last chapter.

Becoming wealthy means learning how to save.

And clearly - you can't save if you have no money to save to begin with.

That's why the Golden Rule is to take care of needs first, wants second.

Here is a very good quote to remember before you buy anything.

"If it isn't a clear YES then it's a clear NO."

So you see a rad tee in a shop window that you really like.

Is buying it there and then a CLEAR yes?

And the key word here is CLEAR.

Because we can all convince ourselves that anything could be a yes: 'I've worked hard', 'I deserve it', 'I haven't bought a new tee shirt for a few weeks', 'it's the summer' etc, etc

So if we have the money, it's very easy to convince ourselves that we could buy it.

But just because we could buy it, doesn't mean we should buy it.

Again - the question to ask ourselves before making any purchase, is "is it a CLEAR yes?"

And here's the thing...

If it is NOT a CLEAR yes - if every fibre of your being is not screaming out "YES I REALLY WANT THIS' - then it's NOT a CLEAR yes - so it's a clear NO.

This statement is a HUGELY powerful filter that will save you time and money.

Use it anytime you are presented with any purchasing option.

So you're going to a party that starts at 7. It's 6 now. Is it a CLEAR yes that you should call an Uber? If it's not a clear yes, then it's a clear no. So call a friend to get a ride or get the bus.

So you're going to see the latest Fast and Furious movie on the big screen.

Is it a CLEAR yes that you spend $20 on popcorn and snacks?

If it's not a clear yes, then it's a clear no.

So go without snacks or bring some candy from home.

So you see a tube of lip gloss that you really want. Is it a CLEAR yes that you purchase it?

Now — maybe it is!

Maybe you've been thinking about this lip gloss all week, and you've been really looking forward to getting it.

In that case, this time it IS a clear YES - so go treat yourself and dip into your savings to make your purchase.

Now it's totally ok to have lots of wants, but the idea is to keep them in check. Think of your wants as chocolate desserts with extra cream.

If you had a chocolate dessert with extra cream all the time, you'd probably get sick of them pretty quick.

But every now and again when you REALLY want one, then that's ok.

Getting good at defining your needs versus your wants is going to provide you with more money to save and invest with.

And the more money you have, the more money you can make.

> **TO SUM UP: The Key Takeaways from this chapter:**
>
> - Needs are things we must have: Wants are things we would like to have
>
> - Take care of your needs first, and wants second
>
> - Before purchasing anything challenge yourself. If it isn't a clear YES then it's a clear NO"

CHAPTER 14:
Investing

"Buy when everyone else is selling and hold until everyone else is buying. It's the very essence of successful investing."
– J. Paul Getty

Let's get one thing clear straight away.

When it comes to the subject of investing there is enough information out there to fill a couple of Yankee Stadiums and a few dozen Hollywood Bowls ....

There are books, events, conferences, talks, retreats, podcasts, seminars and so on and so on this very subject matter.

So, let's cut straight to the chase and keep it simple.

Investing means committing your money to something, with the expectation that this 'thing' will generate a profit for you.

Warren Buffett defines investing as "the process of laying out money now to receive more money in the future."

At its heart, investing is the trading of your money today for a lot more of it in the future.

Now here's the thing.

There are many different types of investments.

You have probably heard of the main types of investments such as Real Estate or the Stock Market.

But there are many other types of investments that you may not have heard of, such as Mutual Funds, Bonds and Options.

All of these are known as Investment Vehicles.

Dividing your money into different kinds of investments is smart. This is called diversification.

When you put your money in different places, you lessen your risk.

The goal of investing is to put your money to work in one or more types of investment vehicle, with the hope of growing your money over time.

Investing done correctly can be jaw-droppingly spectacular.

Because most people spend their time working for money.

You work x hours and get paid y.

But with investments, it's kinda the other way around.

Your money is going out and working for you.

You invest your money in one (or more) of these investment vehicles - and then over time - the investment vehicle (hopefully) increases in value - meaning that by doing literally nothing - your initial investment has also increased in value.

An example would be buying a house.

When you buy a property, you are hoping that after enough time has passed, it will be worth a lot more than you paid for it.

You haven't had to actually do anything to increase the value of your home, except be patient and wait.

So, you are not working for this extra money, the original money you put in to get the home is working and multiplying for you.

Another example is purchasing a Bond. A bond is an investment vehicle from the government. The federal government sells bonds to raise money, which we can then buy, and over time, they will slowly increase in value.

Another example would be buying some shares in a company that is publicly traded.

A publicly traded company means that some of the ownership of the company is dispersed among the general public. In other words - we can own a part of a publicly traded company.

It's quite an amazing feeling to buy some shares and own a part of Nike, or Amazon, or Netflix, or GoPro, or whoever you want. But we can!

Imagine you wanted to own a part of Apple.

So, in this case, we would buy, let's say, $100 worth of Apple shares.

And imagine 12 months later Apple has increased their share price by 10% - meaning we have made a 10% profit on your original investment by doing absolutely nothing.

Now of course - investments can go down as well as up (and often will) - but the general rule of thumb is - if you are patient and are prepared to leave your investments for a long time - you will do well.

Investing is really about "working smarter and not harder."

There are two rules to really stick with when it comes to investing:

1. Play the Long Game.

You really want to invest in something and forget about it. Ideally for at least 5 years (yeah, I know that seems forever but it will go quickly, and all this time, remember you are doing NOTHING while your investment is working for you)

2. Invest What You Can Afford

The key thing with investing is to be strict about what percentage of your money you put aside for your investments.

Just these 2 rules alone will make you a smart and savvy investor.

So many people try to get fancy smancy, but as we've already discussed, simple is always best.

Talking of simple, we have a simple PROCESS that we are going to share with you in the ACCELERATE section - that will make the investing process easy and enjoyable for you to take part in.

So more about that then!

TO SUM UP: The Key Takeaways from this chapter:

- Investing is really about "working smarter and not harder."

- Investing means committing money to an endeavor with the expectation of obtaining an additional income or profit.

- There are many different types of investments including stocks, bonds, real estate, mutual funds and more.

CHAPTER 15:
Stocks & Shares

"Perfection is the enemy of profitability" – anon

So, in the last chapter, we looked at Investments.

In the next couple of chapters, let's look at a few particular types of investment.

And let's start with Shares.

Shares are also known as stocks, they're the same thing.

What is a Stock, or Share?

A stock, or a share, is a unit of ownership in a company.

If you buy a share in Walmart, you have small ownership in Walmart! Yes - you own some of Walmart! Awesome, right?

You are now known as a shareholder.

If the company's profits go up, you 'share' in those profits.

It is a way of making money back that you spend in that business anyway!

If the company's profits fall, so does the price of your stock.

The more involved you get in this, the more exciting and addictive it gets.

Imagine owning some of Microsoft, or IBM, or Walt Disney.

Yes, you can own a part of the company that makes Star Wars! Disney bought the Star Wars brand back in 2012 from its creator George Lucas, for $4.05 billion. Nice one Chewy.

Interestingly as a slight aside - since Disney bought the rights to Star Wars, they have made their original investment back, as the various Star Wars films that have been released since 2012 have made over $4 billion! So, everything they now make from Star Wars will be pure profit that goes in their pocket. The force is strong with them.

Also, as another slight aside – it will never do you any harm to start reading business blogs, or turning on Notifications on your phone from business websites, so you can continually educate yourself as to what is going on in the business world.

Remember - as we said way back at the beginning of this book - the rich know the value of LEARNING.

And that's precisely what you are doing here in this LEARNING section — so respect to you - and let's not get sidetracked but let's carry on!

So, What is the Stock Market?

We all know what a supermarket is for course.   A supermarket is for food what the stock market is for shares.

It's one big place where we can buy and sell shares.

The idea is to buy stock in a company, hold it for a while, and then sell it for a profit.

When it comes to investing, millions of people turn to the Stock Market.

Some people will want to buy shares in companies, others will want to sell.

The Stock Market is in essence where all these deals and trades take place.

It's a meeting place, known as an exchange.

There are more than 140 Stock Exchanges all over the world.

You have probably heard of the more famous Stock Exchanges, such as the New York Stock Exchange (NYSE).

All the most prominent companies that are publicly listed (in other words companies that we can buy and sell shares in) are listed on the NYSE.

Smaller companies that are not big enough to get listed on the NYSE have their own Exchange called the American Stock Exchange (AMEX). AMEX is the second largest stock market in the US (NYSE is #1)

There are also Stock Exchanges that specialize in certain sectors.

For example, there are Stock Exchanges for gold and silver, for precious metals, for oil and gas, even for barley and oats.

Another famous Stock Exchange is the NASDAQ. The NASDAQ is an exchange for over 3000 companies in the 'tech' market.

WHY Does a Company Sell Shares?

As we discussed in the last chapter - we can buy shares in any publicly traded company.

But why would a company sell off part of itself to the public in the first place?

Simple! Because it needs money. Just like everybody!

Businesses really only have 2 main ways to raise money: Borrow money or sell shares.

Many companies will borrow money (which is known as debt financing), but they have to pay it back often with exorbitant interest fees.

However, by selling shares, they can often raise a lot more money, and although they no longer have 100% ownership of their company, they can inject a lot of cash into the business, which may be needed for company expansion, start-up costs, product development etc.

A company will decide what percentage of ownership they will sell to the public.

For example, Facebook is a publicly listed company.

That means that Facebook allows the public to part-own the company.

Mark Zuckerberg who created Facebook still owns the majority stake in his company, but now anyone else can purchase shares meaning if they do they have small ownership in the company too.

Dividends

When we buy shares in a company, we do so most of the time to hold for a while and sell at a later date once the share price has risen and made a profit.

However, some companies will pay you for having stock in them.

This is known as receiving a dividend.

Not every company you invest in will pay dividends, but the older, long established, world-known brands, usually will.

For example, if you purchase shares in Coca-Cola, every year when they announce their profits, a portion of those profits are split equally amongst their shareholders, kind of as a 'thank you' for trusting in them.

This does not affect your original shareholding, you still keep that, a dividend is an additional payment.

Some smart investors live purely on dividends!

They have invested in these more established brands, and they don't touch their original investment, they just let their shares sit there slowly increasing in value over time, while still getting sent checks every year in the form of dividends.

Nice, huh?!

This is a very smart play to make, as you are not touching your original capital (investment) but letting it grow and keeping it for a rainy day.

Bull and Bear Market

One thing we are wanting to do here in *I Need Money* is to encourage you to start thinking like an investor. That means communicating as an investor and using the correct language and terminology.

With that in mind, here are a few more terms that you should be conscious of.

Bull Market And Bear Market.

What are these?

Quite simple, a Bull or Bear is an expression that is often used to describe the current conditions of the Stock Market.

If the market is described as being a BULL - it generally means things are going well or in other words, the prices are going up.

And this is a good thing for the people owning the stocks because their investment has gone up in value.

I'm sure you can guess therefore what a BEAR market is!

You got it when things are not going so well, the market is said to be a BEAR market. Now the prices of most stocks are dropping, and so companies are worth less!

Blue Chip

You may have heard the term 'blue chip' before.

A blue chip company is a long-established, financially stable and historically secure company.

The term "blue chip" comes from the poker world — because in poker a blue chip is the chip that has the highest value.

A blue chip company is considered to be a leading company in its field and produces reliable and often world known goods or services.

Blue chips are usually considered a household name.

Examples of blue chip companies are Apple, Coca-Cola, Disney, IBM and Intel.

They all pay dividends (see above).

The Dow

Because there are so many hundreds of thousands of companies and corporations all trading and all having investors buying and selling shares, it can sometimes be tricky to see at a glance how the overall markets are doing.

To help with this, something called an Index was created.

Essentially an index is a barometer of how the stock market as a whole is doing.

The most famous stock market index is the Dow Jones Industrial Average (DJIA).

When someone asks how the market is doing, most people, journalists, TV outlets, websites etc., quote the DJIA, which is simply referred to as 'the Dow.'

The Dow tracks 30 of the largest and most influential public companies in the stock market, including AT&T, Verizon, Walt Disney, General Motors, ExxonMobil, Home Depot, IBM, Microsoft and McDonalds.

The Dow offers merely an easy-to-understand snapshot of how the stock market is doing, at a glance.

Market Cap

Market capitalization, or 'market cap' as it is often called, is the total dollar (or relevant currency) value of a company.

It allows us to understand the value of one company versus another.

Market cap measures what a company is worth.

It's calculated by multiplying the price of a share by the total number of shares.

For example, imagine a Company X has 10 million shares. And let's imagine the current share price on the Stock Exchange today is $70 per share.

If we multiply 10 million by 70, we get 70 million.

Therefore, as of today, Company X would have a total value of $70million.

It's market cap, therefore, is $70million.

Investors use Market Cap to determine a company's size, as opposed to other metrics like sales, which can change depending on a variety of factors.

It is worth noting that the price of an individual share does not give us any idea how much a company is worth.

You couldn't tell from the price of a share alone what the value of the company is.

The share price simply tells us what the going rate to buy a piece of that company is.

You may also hear the terms large-cap, mid-cap and small-cap.

This simply refers to the market value of a company.

Large-cap companies have a standard market cap of $10 billion or more.

Mid-cap have a market cap of between $2 billion and $10 billion.

And small-cap has a market value anywhere between $250 million to $2 billion.

TO SUM UP: The Key Takeaways from this chapter:

- A stock, or a share, is a unit of ownership in a company.

- The Stock Exchange is where we can buy and sell shares.

- A Bull market means the market is rising. A Bear market means the market is falling

- A blue chip company is a historically secure company.

- The Dow is a barometer of how the stock market is doing as a whole

- Market cap is the total value of a company

CHAPTER 16:
Options

There are other rad things that you can do with the Stock Market when you get a little more educated.

This is a bit more of an advanced strategy, but you can also place a trade that a stock will move in one particular direction during a certain amount of time.

And you don't have to say that a stock will increase, you can make money even if a stock FALLS in value!

Let us explain.

Imagine some bad news is reported about a particular industry.

This could be caused by anything: the environment, something in the news, a natural disaster, a new law being passed, social media, a war etc.

You can then place a trade that a particular stock will fall in value.

And if the stock price does fall, despite the market cap of this company now is worth less, you will MAKE money because you correctly predicted this fall.

As an example, let's imagine there was a national health scare in cattle.

And let's imagine some cattle were found to be diseased and had to be destroyed.

What industries could this affect?

Well, how about the food industry?

This news could affect people wanting to eat beef, as beef, of course, comes from cattle.

So as a result, maybe fewer people visit McDonald's for a while.

Therefore, this health scare that had nothing directly to do with McDonalds could directly impact the price of McDonalds shares.

As an entrepreneur, it's good to start to train ourselves to think like this.

And options trading allows us to capitalize on this.

Options Trading allows us to place a trade on whether we think something will rise or fall.

In the world of Options Trading, if we place a trade that something is going to RISE - that is called a CALL.

If we place a trade that something is going to FALL - that is called a PUT.

You would place a Call or a Put - that a particular stock would RISE or FALL in price - during a certain time interval.

Investors are of course used to making money if a stock rises.

But making money if a stock falls, is a new concept to many.

But that's exactly how Options work!

TO SUM UP: The Key Takeaways from this chapter:

- Options are a type of investment that allow us to make money if a share price rises OR falls, within a specific time period.

- If we place an options trade that something is going to RISE - that is called a CALL.

- If we place an options trade that something is going to FALL - that is called a PUT

CHAPTER 17:
Cultivating Your Entrepreneurial Brain

'Change the way you look at things and the things you look at change.' – Jim Rohn

In the last chapter, we spoke about the power of Options.

Many people are blown away when they learn they can make money if a price FALLS as well as if it rises.

I bet none of your friends knew that. I wonder if your parents and teachers even know that? (ask them!)

This is why EDUCATING yourself on how money works, is so important.

Do you remember back in Chapter 5 when we were talking about Warren Buffett?

Are you beginning to understand why he spends most of his day LEARNING?

Can you see there is a clear correlation between LEARNING and EARNING?

Earning starts with learning.

The way OUT of debt and scarcity that we talked about earlier - and the way INTO abundance and prosperity - starts with learning.

(And don't forget in the next section - in the EARN section - we will be sharing with you EXACTLY how you can make money once you have learned a few of these skills we are going through)

But let's not get too carried away — as we still have a few more things to learn first ☺

And in this chapter, we want to expand upon something we spoke about when we just looked at Options.

In this chapter what we want to share with you an attitude shift that can totally transform your financial situation in a relatively short amount of time.

One of the best skills you can develop as an investor is to be conscious of what is going on around you.

Not just in your neighborhood, but in the world in general.

Being aware of emerging trends, what is becoming popular, what is getting talked about, what is trending on Twitter, what is blowing up on YouTube, what is being blogged about - 'water-cooler' talk as it is known - is a great skill to develop.

In the last chapter, we shared with you an example of how a health scare in cattle would impact the meat and consequently the food industry.

As an entrepreneur, it's good to start to train yourself to think 'how does x affect y?'

Issac Newton once said "for every action, there is an equal and opposite reaction".

That is 100% true.

This means that when anything happens, there will be a reaction to it.

Start to look at what is going on in the business world around you.

If you see a lot of articles about the same topic, stop for a moment and ask yourself what could this increased exposure of this topic that result in?

If there is something that is getting a lot of heat in the news, stop and ask yourself what would be the natural knock-on effect of all this publicity be?

If all your friends are going crazy about a new computer game, switch on your entrepreneurial brain.

Rather than playing the game for hours to try and get the top score, pivot your thinking.

Instead, ask yourself which company makes the game?

If you don't know, research and find out. Google is your friend.

And if that company is a public traded company, maybe it could be wise to explore investing in them. Buy $50 worth of shares maybe?

Are you beginning to see what we are saying here?

We want to train you to start thinking like an entrepreneur.

If everyone is starting to use scooters in your area and it's becoming a booming industry, see who is behind providing them.

If frozen smoothie stalls are popping up all over your State, which company is behind them?

If a new Influencer on YouTube is blowing up and getting millions of views per video, what industry is he/she talking about?

A great way to become rich is to practice opening your eyes to what is going on around you.

Get good at recognizing trends.

For most people - this is a different way of thinking. And will require practice to start thinking in this manner.

But thinking like this is a great skill to master.

Many savvy investors keep an eye sharply on what is going on in the news.

World events can cause many opportunities.

War can cause many stocks to fall, but also many to rise.

So can extreme weather. Extreme sunshine could cause sales of suntan lotion to rocket. That could be a great investment opportunity in the company that makes the lotion!

A country banning something can cause that stock to fall, but you can still make money from this news by placing a PUT options trade (as discussed in the last chapter.)

Do you see what we are doing here?

We want you to start to train yourself to be conscious of what is going on in the world.

A social media video of someone being mistreated on an airplane can go viral and ding the airline's share price.

A celebrity publicly saying something positive about a brand can allow that companies stock to rise.

And you can make money from both.

So, make some changes in your thinking to flex your entrepreneurial muscles.

If you do what you've always done, you're going to get what you've always got.

It will never do you any harm to start reading business blogs or turning on Notifications on your phone from business websites.

Maybe if you're old enough join local entrepreneurs or Business Owners Meet Up Groups, or even start your own.

Benjamin Franklin said it best. "An investment in knowledge pays the best interest,"

TO SUM UP: The Key Takeaways from this chapter:

- Train yourself to be conscious of what is going on in the Business World

- Follow your favorite business topics online; set up notification on your phone or a Google Alert for certain key topics

- When you discover something that is growing in popularity, investigate the brand.

CHAPTER 18:
Assets and Liabilities

"The poor and the middle-class work for money. The rich have money work for them." – Robert Kiyosaki

Assets and Liabilities! Sounds dull, doesn't it?

Well, don't be fooled by the textbook sounding name — because understanding the difference between Assets and Liabilities is the difference between being rich and being poor.

Yes, I said it! It is as big as that!

I thought that would get your attention.

So - what are they?

To put it simply, an ASSET is anything that puts money INTO your pocket.

Whereas a LIABILITY is anything that takes money OUT OF your pocket.

Or to put it another way, assets increase your wealth, while liabilities cost you money.

So - assets - thumbs up.

And - liabilities - thumbs down.

In today's world, if you want to be rich, you have to know the difference between assets and liabilities.

One of the pillars of financial education is the book Rich Dad Poor Dad.

In it, author Robert Kiyosaki says that what makes the rich richer and the poor poorer, is the rich spend their money on assets while the poor spend their money on liabilities.

Things get tricky when we are not sure if something is an asset or a liability.

For example.

Imagine you buy a new car (assuming you are old enough to drive)

And imagine it's going to cost you $300 every month for 5 years.

Is it an asset or a liability?

If you said liability - you'd be correct.

Because it takes money out of your pocket every month.

Now we're not saying you can't have a new car, it's just that the rich know how to turn it into an asset.

Because that's the thing.

Something doesn't have to stay a liability forever. Liabilities can become assets, and assets can become liabilities.

So how can we buy the same car but make it an asset?

Well, we need to have something that is generating us cashflow that we use to pay for the car, rather than relying on our hard earned money in the bank.

This is where Investments (that we discussed in Chapter 14) come into play.

For example, someone may own a building, which pays rent to the owner, and the owner uses some of that rent to pay for the car.

So, the building, and therefore other peoples' money, is paying for your car.

Now the car is an asset.

It's the same with a house.

Most people see their home as an asset.

And here's the thing - it CAN be - but for most people - a house costs them money.

It's taking money OUT of their pocket every month, in the form of the mortgage. Not to mention maintenance, taxes, electricity, water, bills etc.

Therefore - it's a liability.

One of the reasons so many people are struggling financially is because they think they have assets - whereas in fact, in reality, they have liabilities.

A car is a liability. A house is a liability.

What TURNS something into an asset - is something that flows cash into your pocket.

A liability takes money from your pocket.

We're not saying don't buy a house, what we are saying is, can you turn it into an asset?

Maybe you rent out one room. That alone may be enough to cover your mortgage, and so now all of a sudden, your home has gone from being a liability to being an asset.

Now that very same room goes unrented, and costs you money to keep, now the house is back to being a liability again!

So, things can be assets or liabilities - depending on whether they are directly causing money to flow to you.

Stocks can be an asset or a liability, depending on whether they are putting money in your pocket or taking it away.

When you own assets, someone else pays for your lifestyle.

When you own liabilities, you pay for someone else's lifestyle.

Rich people acquire assets.

Poor and middle-class people acquire liabilities, but they think they are assets!

TO SUM UP: The Key Takeaways from this chapter:

- Assets increase your wealth while liabilities cost you money.

- An ASSET is anything that puts money INTO your pocket.

- A LIABILITY is anything that takes money OUT OF your pocket.

CHAPTER 19:
Banks

You may be interested to know the banking system we use today started in Italy approximately 600 years ago, with the oldest bank in the world Banca Monte dei Paschi di Siena and it opened in 1492.

Now, I think it goes without saying we all know what a bank is ☺

A bank, of course, is a place where we can store our money safely.

However - there are a few things about banks that you may not be aware of.

Firstly — have you ever wondered how a bank makes its money?

Well, here's how, and it's fascinating.

Banks encourage us to leave as much money as possible with them.

They incentivize us to do this, by paying us a small amount of money called 'interest'.

The more money we have in our bank account, the more interest the bank pays us.

However - don't get too excited - because whereas this is 'free money' - the interest rate is always a tiny %. But still, it's better than a punch in the face, right?

So, why does the bank want us to leave money with them?

Well, this is how they make THEIR money.

Banks lend out OUR money - to other people.

Say, what?

Yes - you did read that correctly!

They take OUR money - that we work hard for - and that we give them to look after - and then they take it (without asking us) and lend it to people who want a loan.

But wait, there's more.

The bank then charges a HIGHER interest rate to those they have loaned the money to - than they pay us in interest - for this privilege.

The cheek of it!

But think about it - everybody benefits.

We have peace of mind that our money is safe and accessible.

The bank has a continual influx of money that they can then lend out and charge for.

And people that want loans (such as mortgages, car loans etc.) can always access funds because of the huge pool of money within the banking system.

Win, win, win.

As account holders, we can open different types of bank accounts — and there are benefits and drawbacks to each.

Current/Checking Account

A current or checking account is where most people keep their salary.

It is the account that their employer pays their money into.

It is also the account that most people pay their bills out of like their mortgage, car loan, grocery bills, heating, gas bills and so on.

Funnily enough, many adults continue to use the bank account that they had opened for them when they were children!

There are however a lot smarter ways to run your bank accounts, which we will be coming onto in the ACCELERATE section.

One of the many advantages of a checking account is you can access your money at any time 24/7 using ATM/Cash machines anywhere on the planet no matter where your account was opened.

An ATM machine is an Automated Teller Machine sometimes more easily described as a "cashpoint".

They have existed since the 1960's and have made money really easy to access.

This was not always the way.

Up until relatively recently, you could only withdraw money from ATM machines in the country that you had your bank account, but this has all changed.

Savings Account

The next type of account you can open is a savings account, and this is the easiest account to open for children or teens.

The advantage of a savings account is that it pays you a higher rate of interest than a current account.

The disadvantage is that it is not as easy to get your money out at short notice.

You generally need to give the bank notice of withdrawal in advance by a few days, if not longer.

There are also more long-term savings accounts where you lock your money away for months or even years, and also investment accounts and we will discuss these in ACCELERATE.

As we mentioned earlier, one of the interesting things about banks is that they do not keep your money in the bank; most of it they have given away as loans.

If everyone showed up at the same time looking for their money, the money is not there!

Banks only hold between 3% and 10% of the money deposited there which means every now and again when people get a bit panicked about this fact, we have what is known as a "bank run" when everyone tries to get their money at once which sometimes results in the banks going out of business.

This is extremely rare, but it has happened!

As a result, in most countries, the government places a guarantee on the money in accounts to a certain limit, to help people feel less stressed about the fact that their money is not where they think it is!

TO SUM UP: The Key Takeaways from this chapter:

- Banks make their money by lending out our money and charging interest on this loan

- The 2 most common types of bank accounts are a Checking Account and a Savings Account

CHAPTER 20:
Credit & Credit Cards

One of the main differences between the rich and the poor is how they make use of credit.

Credit is borrowing.

And if you borrow money, you owe someone a debt.

There's that word again - debt.

Remember in Chapter 11 when we talked about the 5 levels of wealth?

Remember the very bottom level? The level that we want to avoid, yet ironically the level that MOST people are constantly in?

It was DEBT.

One of the reasons for this - is credit cards.

Using a credit card is really taking out a loan.

With a credit card, you are spending money you don't have!

You are in borrowing money from the bank without ever having to pay them a visit!

In other words, you are borrowing money from tomorrow that you don't have to get by today!

To get a credit card, you must apply to the company or bank, and they will have some criteria that you will need to meet to be allowed to receive one.

As soon as you receive it, they issue you with a "credit limit" which means you can only spend to a maximum of that limit.

You are then expected to pay this money back within a predefined period of time.

These credit limits often get raised, which may sound great, but all that really happens is people have access to more money they can spend, and most people do, trapping them forever with trying to pay it back.

And of course, we are charged a very high rate of interest on what we borrow.

Some credit cards have an interest rate as high as 30%.

This means that for you to borrow $100, you have to pay back $130.

It is definitely not the most cost effective way of getting a loan, but people love credit cards because of their convenience.

It is very easy however to fall into the trap of increasing debt, where you owe a lot more money than you have in a very short space of time.

The real problem with credit cards is how easy they are to use!

It doesn't even feel like you're spending money!

One swipe here, another there, and things add up.

Do that enough times in a month, and SURPRISE!

Look at that credit card balance you now owe. Where did it come from?

I'll tell you where it came from.

It came from that night when after you went bowling with your friends you grabbed some pizza. $24.

Then there was that amazing jacket reduced from $135 to $74 that you couldn't pass up on. $74.

Don't forget the new albums from Panic at the Disco, Twenty One Pilots and Drake that you bought. $35.

Then there was that Saturday afternoon at the Mall. Not sure exactly what you bought but all in it came to $68.

You get the general idea.

Suddenly, you've now got over $200 on your credit card.

How did that happen?

Well, as we've said, and as MANY people discover the hard way, it is way way way too too too easy to spend money on your credit card.

So, suddenly you are in debt.

Most people can't afford to pay off their entire credit card bill every month, so imagine you pay off the minimum, which let's say is $25.

Now you are being charged interest on your debt of $175.

Then one month you don't make a payment, so you are charged a 'late fee' of $30. And you're interest rate is 17.5%, which is about another $30. So after month one, you have $60 in fee's, so you now owe $235.

I'm sure you can see where this is going.

Now you owe more than you borrowed! Plus interest will keep being added every month.

It's a very slippery slope, and most people get caught in this.

Making a few bad choices when using credit cards can wipe out savings and build debt.

Credit cards, therefore, are best used for purchases that can be paid off each month.

Remember in Chapter 18 here in *I Need Money* when we spoke about assets and liabilities?

Well, using credit cards to purchase liabilities, which take money out of your pockets like clothes or a holiday or a car, is a very bad idea.

However, if you use a Credit Card to fund an asset like education on how to build a business, now that could prove to be a very wise decision.

If you are going to constantly use a Credit Card (and we'd advise against it) but if you do, try and pay back loans on time, because not only will you avoid paying interest, but the banks will assign you with a very good credit history score.

This is a signal to other banks and lending institutions that you are to be trusted when it comes to applying for a new loan.

If on the other hand, you are really bad at paying back loans, things only get worse for you as you are issued with a very poor credit score.

A bad credit score can follow you around for years and can impact everything, from the mortgage rate you will get offered when you purchase a house, to if you will be accepted to open a Store Card at Banana Republic (and imagine the embarrassment of getting turned down at Banana Republic) (just kidding Banana Republic, we love you really…)

So what happens if you want to buy something but you don't have the money for it, but you have a Credit Card?

Simple.

You don't buy it.

So you want the new iPhone?

Most poor people would tell you to put it on your Credit Card.

But that's why they are poor.

The Rich Person will tell you if you can't afford it without putting it on your credit card - then don't get it.

That's right.

Don't buy it! Wait!

You WAIT until you have the money, and then you buy it.

Instead, EARN the money, and then spend it on the iPhone.

But HOW do you earn the money you may be asking?

Well, we're glad you asked!

Let me remind you - our entire EARN section here in *I Need Money* is dedicated to sharing with you 37 different ways that you can make money.

And we'll be at EARN, very soon young jedi.

TO SUM UP: The Key Takeaways from this chapter:

- One of the main differences between the rich and the poor, is how they make use of credit.

- Poor people put purchases on their credit cards and make minimum payments every month getting trapped with the high-interest fees often for years

- Rich people will either not use a Credit Card at all if they can't afford the item, or they will use a Credit Card but pay off the full balance every month, therefore, avoiding the high-interest fees

CHAPTER 21:
Debit Cards

Debit cards are a different beast completely to their credit card cousins.

Although they look the same, there is a massive difference between the two!

The main difference is that with the debit card you are spending money you have while with a credit card you are spending money you don't have!

Debit cards are a piece of plastic with a unique chip that you are given when you open a new current account.

It allows you to withdraw money directly from ATM machines from the account you opened which we described earlier, or you can use them to pay for products or services directly in a shop or online, like for booking a flight for example.

The main thing to note about a debit card is that it allows you to spend money that you already have in your account.

If you do not have enough money in your account and you try to withdraw more from the ATM machine or to use it in a shop, they will tell you that there are "insufficient funds" which means you are all out of mula!

Sometimes your bank can charge you for each time you use your debit card at an ATM - but ideally, you should look for a bank that doesn't do this. It is your money after all!

When you receive a debit card in the mail, a few days later you are sent a separate letter that gives you a unique PIN number (Personal Identification Number) which only allows people who have both the pin number and the card to use the card.

It is highly recommended that you then change the PIN number that the bank gives you to something else that you can remember and then throw away the piece of paper you received.

You should never write down your pin number anywhere near your card for security reasons.

More recently debit cards have had a new feature added to them which allows you to use them without even needing a PIN number.

You can just tap them against the processing machine for the money to be taken.

There is a limit on how much you can spend on these cards without using a PIN number for safety reasons.

Debit cards are not as 'dangerous' as Credit Cards, as you are only spending money that you have, as opposed to borrowing money that you don't.

But even so, you want to be careful that you don't go too crazy with your debit cards.

If on the one hand, you are going to be slowly but surely building up your bank account....

...you don't want on the other hand, to be emptying it due to aggressive use of a Debit Card!

TO SUM UP: The Key Takeaways from this chapter:

- A Debit Card allows you to easily spend money that you already have

- A Debit Card is linked to your bank account.

- Any transaction on your Debit Card automatically withdraws that amount from your bank.

CHAPTER 22:
Profit & Loss

Profit is good!

Loss is bad!

That's it for this chapter.

Just kidding.

Anyone that is financially successful understands what their Profit and Loss is.

And it's a very simple concept, but interestingly, a lot of people shy away from it.

But there is no need.

A profit and loss (P&L) statement is a financial statement that summarizes the incomes and expenses, and leftover balances, incurred during a specified period.

Well, structured businesses will have P&L statements every year, most will have P&L statements every quarter, and these days a lot will have monthly P&L.

Here's the thing. You can't improve anything that you don't measure.

Forget business for a moment, that statement is true for anything in life.

Think about it, if you lift weights and you want to get stronger, you can't improve if you don't know the numbers of what you are currently lifting.

If you're a sprinter, you will know your numbers for how long it takes you to run 200m.

And so, it is the same financially.

We can't improve what we don't measure.

Financial intelligence includes measuring what is coming in, what is going out, and what you are keeping.

Remember, in the EARN section here we are going to be showing you many specific ways that you can make money.

You will want to develop the healthy habit of tracking what you are making and what you are spending.

This is where a P&L statement comes in handy.

A profit and loss statement shows the actual profit for your business, or, it may show the loss for your business if things are not doing as well as you hoped.

But it's powerful to see your numbers written down.

The math doesn't lie!

Many people, particularly when they are starting out, often think things are going better than they are.

They may have made a bit of money, but often have 'forgotten' about some costs, that when factored in, do in fact reduce the profits.

Being good at P&L prevents this - and gives us a foundation to build upon.

A P&L statement does not need to be complicated.

At the very least, all it needs to have is:

1. The total income you have made that month BEFORE any expenses/ costs (this is known as GROSS income)

2. A detailed breakdown of all your expenses/costs

3. The money remaining AFTER your expenses/cost (this is known as NET income)

So, let's imagine you have created a part-time business that you run at weekends, washing neighbors cars.

Apart from this being a very lucrative thing to do, as a business owner, you need to get good at the 'accounting' part of your business.

I know most people find this boring, everybody does to an extent, but you are the BOSS! It's important therefore to spend a few minutes getting your head around this and knowing your numbers.

Here is how a simple P&L statement could look for your business.

P&L Statement for July - for WashMyNeighbors Cars

INCOME:

Total number of cars washed in July:	21
Total income (including tips) for July:	$392
GROSS PROFIT:	$392
EXPENSES:	
Wages (my brother Dave):	$100
3 buckets:	$21
Pack of sponges	$ 10
Turtle wax:	$16
Gloves:	$10
Total Expenses:	**$158**
NET PROFIT:	**$234**

So, as you can see from this example, just getting into the habit of documenting everything, makes it super easy to see at a glance what is going on in your business.

This is the cornerstone of any future growth.

Now you can see what is going on where you have a foundation to grow from.

You can budget that with the above figures, after your costs, you can expect to pocket a rather handsome figure of about $234/month.

That's $234 you can invest, save, and grow (which we will explain how to do in ACCELERATE)

It's actually exhilarating to get organized and to see your P&L statement - particularly the first time you do this.

It makes things 'real'.

As we move into the EARN section, we will be coming back to documenting your income and expenses, so more about that very soon.

TO SUM UP: The Key Takeaways from this chapter:

- A profit and loss statement is a financial statement that summarizes the incomes and expenses during a specified period.

- Income before any deductions/expenses is known as GROSS income

- Income after deductions/expenses is known as NET income

CHAPTER 23:
Employee vs Business Owner

Just checking in! How are you feeling?

Still feeling good? Still feeling pumped?

We do hope so, as we are getting very close to the EARN section now.

We still have a few things to share with you though, and in this chapter, we want to briefly share with you the following.

Did you know there are many types of workers in the world?

Often times, they are usually categorised into two simple segments.

The first are those who work for others and have a boss.

Secondly there are workers who own businesses often known as business owners!

In reality there are more than just these two.

Until you understand that there are actually a number of stages, you may end up like many people owning a business (in theory) but end up working just as hard in this business as you did when working for someone else.

In chapter 40, we will introduce you to what we call the JEDI model which shows that there are in fact four stages to "work" our way through.

Before getting to that, there is a much simpler question to ask first; would you prefer to work for someone else or for yourself?

The truth is that it may not be as easy to answer as it seems.

Being a job owner or employee (working for someone else) or working for yourself sometimes known as self employed can both be very tough and involve a lot of long hours.

However taking the step to becoming self employed is definitely in the right direction but not where we recommend you stay in the long term.

Only very few people will ever become rich by working for others, and generally they must work their way up to the very top of the organization.

The vast majority of the wealthy start with being self employed but rapidly move to owning the business as opposed to working themselves.

A lot of people are confused between being self employed and owning a business which creates a lot of long term frustration but we will fix this with the JEDI model.

And as we have said a few times now, in the EARN section here, we are going to share with you STEP BY STEP many business ideas to ignite that entrepreneurial fire inside you that will you get you started in business.

In fact, we are almost at the EARN section.

Just before we get to it though — just a few more things to run through here in LEARN.

TO SUM UP: The Key Takeaways from this chapter:

- Employees work for someone else.

- Self employed and being a business owner are not necessarily the same thing. One involves working in a business while the other involves working on the business.

- Neither employee (job owner) nor self employed are recommended for where we want to be in the long term.

CHAPTER 24:
Tax (Made Fun, Honest...)

"There are only two things certain in life: death and taxes" – Benjamin Franklin

Urggghhhhhhhhhhhhhhhh.

Tax?

Really?

Kill me now.

Could there be anything duller?

Look, we geddit. Reading about tax is about as exciting as a trip to school for an exam in your least favorite subject.

But, give us just a few minutes okay? That's all.

Remember making money STARTS with LEARNING.

And as tax is such a big chunk of business, we need to at least get through the fundamentals.

And we'll try to emphasize the FUN part of that. Deal? Okay, let's carry on...

Tax is always going to be the biggest deduction on your NET Income.

It is the biggest bill in your entire life!!

But the golden rules are made by the people with the gold ... that's you very soon!

Remember - NET income is what you make after all your deductions.

So, in our Car Wash example in Chapter 22, our Net Income was $234/month.

If that were consistent, that would work out at $2808/year.

And so that is approximately the figure that you would pay tax on.

I say approximately because tax laws are complicated.

We can earn a certain amount tax-free. Then as soon as we earn over that, we are taxed at a certain rate. Then again, when we make more than a certain amount, the tax rate will change again.

There's a saying that you may have heard of.

There are only two certainties in life, death and taxes.

That's pretty much true,

Now there are loopholes to reduce tax, and you can even move to certain countries in the world where there is NO tax to pay (but you'll have to keep your money in that country) - but for all intents and purposes - you WILL be paying tax in your life.

And tax has nothing to do with age.

If you are making the tax payments threshold, it doesn't matter your age, you will owe tax.

One thing that is worth mentioning is, whereas a lot of people don't like tax, it's important to remember where it goes.

Tax goes to the government or your state, and it helps to pay for the running of the country/state.

Think about it, who pays for and builds the roads that we drive on, who pays for the electricity that lights the streets at night?

Who pays for transportation, who pays for airports and train stations?

Who pays for the police force, the fire service, rangers, medical emergency services, schools, colleges, the welfare system etc. etc. etc.

Have you ever stopped to ask yourself this?

Most people have not.

You get the general idea!

Without getting into a heated debate about where our money should go, long story short, our taxes get reinvested into the country to pay for things that benefit us.

We know it can be painful having to pay taxes, but it's important to remember that we do indirectly benefit from it!

Tax laws, of course, vary from country to country.

In countries such as the UK, you pay Income Tax to the Government.

But in the US, you pay taxes to two places. You pay Federal Tax (i.e. a National Tax), and on top of that you pay a tax to your state (State Tax).

One of the many advantages in having your own business - is you can 'offset' any business expense.

For example, imagine you have a part-time Saturday business selling cakes.

And imagine you make $150 GROSS every Saturday.

Do you remember what GROSS means?

Well done if you did without having to scroll back! Gross means how much you make BEFORE any deductions.

So, if we are making $150 gross, there will be some expenses.

Imagine we have $50 of expenses.

That means our NET profit is $100 ($150 gross minus the $50 expenses)

Remember - NET means how much we make AFTER our expenses have been deducted.

Now here's the cool thing.

We only get taxed on our NET figure.

So, in this case, we'd only be taxed on $100. Not $150. So, we are still paying tax, but it's less than you may have at first thought.

Also - over the years that you are in business - you will learn that there are MANY other tax benefits.

By far one of the most attractive is that anything you do that is clearly for your business - you can 'write off' as a business expense.

So, that means whatever that expense is, you don't pay tax on it.

Let's imagine in a few years one of your businesses is really beginning to do well.

And let's imagine you have the opportunity to fly to San Francisco to meet with a possible future business contact.

Your flight, your hotel, even your food that you have on the trip - can all be deducted from your business and counted as an expense.

That means you can hugely reduce your tax bill, by running lots of legitimate things through your business.

I know we are getting a bit ahead of ourselves, but being the entrepreneur that you are - this is useful information for you to at least store in your head.

Very soon (if not already now) you'll find yourself wondering why people get a JOB - when there are so many more exciting opportunities to create your own business.

So - you still awake? ☺

Good.

There - this whole tax thing wasn't THAT boring was it?

Just 2 more quick tax things you should know.

TAX Return

If you have your own business, every year you will need to fill in a Tax Return.

This is where having been diligent with your Profit and Loss statements (as discussed in Chapter 22) will really help - as you will already have all the figures handy.

In the US - you will file two tax returns.

One to the government (your Federal return) and one to your State (your State return).

You do not send any money with your Tax Return - you are just telling the authorities how much you have made.

Essentially you are sharing your Profit and Loss statement for the year with the authorities.

When you hear people talk about 'filing their taxes' they are talking about completing their tax return and sending it off.

It's worth mentioning that only Business Owners have to fill in a Tax Return.

Most people have a JOB. But that's what most people are in debt or in scarcity.

Anyone who has a job will not have to fill in a tax return, as the company they work for will pay their taxes.

And employees of a company will get a paycheck every month that will list their gross and net pay. An employee can't do anything about any of the figures.

Tax Bill

Your tax bill is how much you actually pay.

As we discussed in the last chapter, if you are an employee you will not get a tax bill, as the company you work for will take care of your payroll and pay your taxes for you.

But if you are a Business Owner, you will have your own Tax Bill to pay. Or maybe two if you're in the US (Federal and State)

One final quick thing to mention about Tax Bills, and that is Estimated Taxes.

It can be very advantageous to pay Estimated Taxes every 3 months during the year.

In fact, depending on how much you make, you may have to do this (I say 'have' - it's not a law, but you are strongly encouraged to do so)

Paying estimated taxes is good, as it gives you a real grasp on where you are in your business, plus you don't get one 'big' tax bill once a year, but smaller more comfortable to manage payments split up throughout the year.

Ok, you can stop looking longingly at your PS4, we're done with taxes ☺

And we're almost done with LEARN. Just a few quick more information grenades to throw in, starting with Passive Income vs Linear Income, which is something you WILL be amped up about.

Let's jump into that next...

TO SUM UP: The Key Takeaways from this chapter:

- There are only two certainties in life, death and taxes

- In the US you will pay Federal Tax to the Government, and State Tax to your State

- Employees have their tax paid for them by their JOB: Business Owners have to file and pay their taxes themselves

CHAPTER 25:
Passive Income vs Linear Income

"Work smarter, not harder"
– Allen F. Morgenstern

It's time to share something with you that will completely change how you look at money.

Only the rich understand what you are about to discover.

Ready?

And it has to do with something called Passive Income and Linear Income.

Let us explain…

Linear Income

Over 90% of people earn Linear Income.

What this means, is they trade their time for money.

I other words, they have a JOB.

They most likely commute, go to an office, and spend at least 40 hours per week working in that office for a fixed paycheck.

If they stop working, the money stops.

That is most people's lives.

This is known as earning LINEAR INCOME.

You give your TIME, and in return you get a certain amount of MONEY.

But here's the kicker.

You will never get wealthy like this.

I repeat. You will never get wealthy like this.

Most people are making Linear Income.

Which makes sense, as most people are in debt or living in scarcity.

That's the bad news.

Wanna hear the good news?

There is a way out.

And it's the opposite of Linear Income.

Passive Income

The opposite of Linear Income is called Passive Income.

It's also known as Residual Income.

Once you understand Passive income, you will never want to have anything to do with Linear Income again!!

Passive Income is the most powerful and profitable source of income.

Passive Income is the income of the rich.

Passive Income means that you set something up once - or you do some work once - but you continue to get paid for it, time and time again.

You 'set and forget' if you like.

Now, don't get us wrong, just like anything it will still require a bit of hard work at first to set this thing up, but once you put in some sweat equity, determination and hard graft, then the magic of Passive Income can start working.

The Ultimate goal of having your own business is to have some sort of Passive Income component to it.

Even if you have a business that requires you to be hands on, there is no reason why down the line, you can't create some sort of Passive Income element to it.

For example - imagine you created a business during your summer vacation of mowing people's lawns.

After a bit of hard work setting it all up, imagine you get paid $35 per lawn.

What's to stop you after a while hiring a reliable friend of yours to do the work, and pay them, maybe $20.

In this case, you are making $15/lawn passive income, as you are having to do nothing (after of course the initial hard work of setting everything up) but still generating some income.

Once you get your head around Passive Income, you will realize that's all you want to focus on.

There are many different examples of Passive Income.

- Selling products online. You do the work once and focus on getting traffic to your website to make sales (this is known as eCommerce)

- Any investment (stocks,shares,options etc) that make you money are making you Passive Income

- Having a rental property. The income you make from renting it out is passive income. You are not spending your time working for it.

- Have your own YouTube channel. If you get enough views you can have ads show before and during your videos, and get a split of how much these ads make

- Create an App. Once it's created and selling, all the money you make after your costs is passive income

Most people were brought up being told to get a job.

This is an outdated formula for creating wealth.

A JOB will result in Linear Income.

The key is to spend your time doing what the rich already know.

And that is focusing on Passive Income activities.

It's the exact opposite of linear income!

Other examples of Passive income include:

- Writing a book. If copies continue to sell years after the book was published, the author continues to get paid for something that he worked on once way back when.

- Writing music. Many musicians continue to make money on songs years after they were released.

- Sales from ads that are earned through a blog or website

- Interest paid on a savings account

It's also worth noting that the income stream from Passive Income can often be large enough to live comfortably on, allowing for more opportunities to try new things, travel and explore new business ideas.

So, which should you be focusing on? Linear or Passive income?

If you said Passive — congratulations!

(and if you said Linear, read this chapter again!)

TO SUM UP: The Key Takeaways from this chapter:

- There are two types of income. Passive Income and Linear Income.

- Linear income is trading your time for money. You work x hours and get paid y.

- Passive Income means that you set something up once - or you do some work once - but you continue to get paid for it time and time again.

CHAPTER 26:
Good Debt vs Bad Debt

Debt is a 4 lettered word for most people.

In 2016 in the US, the average household had a credit card debt of $16,784.

The average person in the US pays over $600,000 in interest on debt in a lifetime!

We've already discussed how most people live in debt.

However - would it surprise you if I said there is such a thing as Good Debt as well a Bad Debt?

Let's explore both.

And let's start with the type of debt that most people are familiar with — Bad Debt.

Bad Debt

Anything that decreases in value the minute after you buy it is bad debt.

Unfortunately, that describes many of life's basic necessities, like clothes, cars and electronics.

High-interest credit card purchases are bad debt.

Plastic can ruin your financial health, and interest rates are the silent killer.

Of course, most people need a credit card as it's just convenient, and we are not saying don't use credit cards.

What we are saying is pay off the balance on your Credit Card every month.

It's keeping a balance and therefore getting charged and those high-interest rates that cripple most people.

Other examples of bad debt include taking on a loan for a vacation or new clothes.

Car loans are generally considered bad debt because the value of your car will fall as soon as you drive off the forecourt.

On the other hand, most people do need cars and maybe can't afford to buy one outright.

So, the interest on car loans is generally quite low, but even so, if you can afford not to go into debt to make the purchase, that would be the best option of all.

Or as we discussed in Chapter 18 here in, *I Need Money*, invest in an asset that generates an income that you can use to cover the cost of monthly repayments for the car.

However, none of the debts above are nearly as brutal as Payday loans.

Payday Loans are arguably the worst debt to get into.

And worryingly, Payday Loans can be seen on most High Streets.

A Payday loan will give you a short-term loan to help you through a tough spot financially.

Loan amounts vary from $50 to as much as $1,000 depending on the law.

If approved, you receive cash on the spot.

Full payment is due on the borrower's next payday, which typically is around two weeks.

Borrowers either post date a personal check to coincide with their next paycheck or give the payday lender electronic access to withdraw funds from the customer's bank account.

Payday loans charge up to $15 to $30 for every $100 borrowed, which can work out as high as a staggering 400% interest rate.

However, get this, the Consumer Financial Protection Bureau says 80% of payday loans don't get paid back in two weeks.

That means they get 'rolled over' into the following month, increasing the interest rate even more to a stratospherically high 521%, and will continue to rise every time the debt is not paid.

You can see how many people ended up getting trapped.

Many people think that a Payday loan is a quick short-term fix when in a tight spot, but the reality is they are often a budget-busting experience for most that get involved.

And 20% end up in default, which goes on your credit report for seven years and all but eliminates you from getting credit in the near future.

Default also opens you up to harassment from debt collection agencies, who either buy the loan from the payday lender or are hired to collect it.

Either way, it's an awful experience to go through.

Let's change the conversation, shall we?

How about we look at Good Debt?

Good Debt

Good debt is any debt that allows you to manage your finances more effectively.

For example, buying things that save you time and money.

Investing in education is seen as good debt.

Yes, you may go into debt to LEARN something, but the skills you are learning will make you more valuable long-term - making you more valuable and therefore hopefully allowing you to make more money.

Another good debt is taking out a mortgage.

Again, yes you are now in debt, but you have invested in something that not only will be your home, but also that will hopefully increase over time.

A loan to set up a business is seen as good debt, as you are using the money to build a business and hopefully make a lot more money in the long term.

Interestingly - Student Loans sort of fall into a grey area.

Some people call Student Loans good debt - as the debt is regarded as an investment in your future and student loans tend to have lower interest rates.

However, some people call them bad debt as it's entirely possible to come out of school owing hundreds of thousands of dollars, which naturally can take 10,15, sometimes 20 years to pay off.

For example, studying to become a doctor takes on average 5 years and can quickly rack up $500,000 worth of debt. Imagine how long it would take to pay off $500,000....

As with any debt, the idea is to clear it as soon as possible, and that's what we will be going through in EARN.

TO SUM UP: The Key Takeaways from this chapter:

- Good debt can help you achieve goals, while bad debt is expensive and can derail them.

- Anything that decreases in value the minute after you buy it is bad debt.

- Good debt is any debt that allows you to save your time and money

CHAPTER 27:
Compounding Interest

"Make thy gold multiply"
— The Richest Man in Babylon

Einstein.

He kinda knew a thing or two, didn't he?

And I mean the mathematician and physicist by the way, not the dog out of Back To The Future.

Einstein is generally regarded as one of the smartest peeps ever.

He won the Nobel Prize.

He made many discoveries.

He came up with the theory of relativity and E=MC².

However, he also described the topic of this chapter as 'the most powerful force in the universe'.

So - if the smartest brain even said this - we should take note, right?

Einstein was talking about something called Compound Interest.

In fact, Einstein went on to say that "Compound interest is the eighth wonder of the world. He who understands it earns it ... he who doesn't ... pays it"

So, the most powerful force in the Universe, right?

Well, if Einny said that, we should probably listen.

Now - here's there thing - because Compounding Interest is SO IMPORTANT - we are going to come back to it in more detail in ACCELERATE.

But for now - let us give you the overview as to what Compounding Interest is.

Compounding Interest allows us to earn interest, on our interest.

What?

I know, I know, it can be confusing.

So, let's really break this down.

To do this lets firstly explain 'normal' interest or simple interest as it is known.

Simple Interest

For the sake of this illustration, let's keep the numbers simple.

Imagine you have $1,000, and you put it in the bank.

And imagine it earns 10% interest in a year.

That means after a year you have made $100 in interest.

Plus, you still have your original investment of $1,000.

So now in total, after a year, you have $1,100.

Pretty straightforward, right?

Now - a lot of people will take the extra money they have made, in this case, the $100 - because it's free money.

So, you could easily withdrawal the $100 you made in interest, and spend it on what you want, and you STILL have your original $1,000 in the bank.

Then in year 2, the process starts again.

That means after a year, you will have made another $100 in interest. So, you are back at $1,100 in total again.

And again - if you want - you can take the interest to spend.

And so, this process can repeat forever, you making free money every year on your initial investment.

So, that's Simple Interest.

But what then, is Compounding?

Compounding Interest

Let's use the same example above, this time using Compounding Interest.

So, we have our $1,000, and we put it in the bank.

It earns 10% interest in a year.

After a year you have therefore made $100 in interest.

Plus, you still have your original investment of $1,000.

So, just like with Simple Interest, after a year, we now have $1,100 in total.

Now, here's where it gets different with Compounding.

With Compounding, we do not touch the interest, but we keep it and add it to our original investment.

So instead of removing the $100 to spend, with Compounding, we keep it where it is moving into Year 2.

This means in the 2nd year, we have a principal investment now of $1,100.

Again, let's imagine we get 10% interest on this.

So now we are earning 10% on our new figure of $1,100, as opposed to the $1,000 with Simple Interest.

10% of $1,100 is $110.

We have now made a bit more money in our second year with compounding versus with simple.

Now at the end of the 2nd year, we add this interest that we have made ($110) to our principal which was now $1,100, and so now by the end of year two, we have $1,210.

Essentially what we are doing here is reinvesting our interest every year, thereby increasing our principal, meaning we will make more interest on it.

Here's the thing - this can make a HUGE difference to how much money you have.

Over time, our money will grow a lot faster than if we just had 'simple' interest.

This growth is referred to as the "time value of money."

The biggest mistake that most people make is they fail to take advantage of the incredible power of compounding.

The multiplying power of growth x growth.

There is a reason that Albert Einstein was so revved up about it!

We will come back to Compounding Interest more in Accelerate.

TO SUM UP: The Key Takeaways from this chapter:

- Compounding Interest means reinvesting interest, rather than paying it out

- Compound interest allows us to earn interest on the interest, as well as the original principal.

- Albert Einstein called it 'the most powerful force in the universe.'

CHAPTER 28:
Cryptocurrency

Cryptocurrency is the current buzzword.

Everybody is talking about it, everybody has an opinion on it.

But what exactly is cryptocurrency?

Long story short, it is Digital Money.

Unlike conventional coins and cash, there is nothing tangible with Cryptocurrency.

That means cryptocurrency does not have physical form. It's money but in digital form.

There are thousands of different types of cryptocurrency.

The most famous is Bitcoin that I am sure you have heard of.

Bitcoin was created in 2009, by a mysterious person called Satoshi Nakamoto.

Nobody knows for sure if that is a real person or the name given to a group of people.

Regardless of who (or what!) Satoshi may be, Bitcoin has ballooned in popularity (and price) in the last few years.

Anyone can buy Bitcoin. We do this at an Online Cryptocurrency Exchange of which there are many.

The largest is Coinbase.

After verifying your identity, you can use your Credit Card or Bank Account to purchase Bitcoin.

Just like stocks and shares, the price of Bitcoin (and indeed all Coins and Tokens) change in price every day. In fact, the price is often very volatile.

Another term that you will often hear in the Cryptoworld is altcoins.

An altcoin is any digital cryptocurrency similar to Bitcoin.

The term stands for "alternative to Bitcoin". At the time of writing this book, there are almost 2000 ltcoins. Over time, it's expected that many will cease to exist.

Once we buy any Cryptocurrency, it is stored in a digital wallet.

To pay for something in Crypto, firstly we have to make sure that they take crypto as a payment method.

More and more people and companies are, but it is still very new and has not yet reached mass adoption in the world. In fact mass adoption is still years away, and possibly may never happen.

But if a company does accept Crypto, all we do is log into our Online Wallet and punch in their address, choose how much money to send, press a button, and that's it.

The transaction is pretty much instantaneous.

TO SUM UP: The Key Takeaways from this chapter:

- Cryptocurrency is Digital Currency
- There are thousands of different Crypto Coins or tokens and they are also known as altcoins
- The most famous Cryptocurrency is Bitcoin

CHAPTER 29:
LEARN – Wrapping Up

The way to success is through the continuous pursuit of knowledge.

Wealthy people are not wealthy because of some complex strategy.

They are wealthy because they do things that other people are not prepared to do.

The foundation for building any sort of wealth is spending time wisely in EDUCATION.

So, well done for going through LEARN here in *I Need Money*.

Now, we suggest you put this book down, take some time out, and get energized, because in the next Section - we are moving onto EARN.

Now we have learned some skills here in LEARN, how can we use them to make money?

That's precisely what we are going to go through in EARN.

See you there next!

SECTION 5: EARN

www.funancialfreedom.com

CHAPTER 30:
EARN – Introduction

"To change one's life: Start immediately. Do it flamboyantly. No exceptions" – William James

Let me tell you about Tony Hsieh.

In 1999, Tony had an idea to sell shoes online.

He called his company Zappos.

10 years later, Tony sold Zappos to Amazon for 1 billion dollars.

Yes, billion. With a b.

Tony is a great guy to learn from when it comes to creating a business and making a lot of money from it.

And he once said something that is excellent advice for us all.

He said, "don't play games you don't understand."

What he means is don't attempt to do anything until you really understand what it is you are doing.

Many people lose money because they don't know what they are doing.

They are playing games they don't understand.

Sure, they want to be wealthy, but wealth is the end result.

And we can't start at the end.

We need to know how to get there. We need a roadmap.

And that's precisely what we have for you here in EARN.

This is your roadmap.

Here in EARN, we are going to share with you 37 different ways that you can start earning straight away.

Within those 37, we're going to pick 4 randomly and dig into a deeper dive.

By the way, we go into detail in all of the 37 ways you can start earning, at our website www.funancialfreedom.com.

So, without further ado, let us share with you 37 Ways That You Can Start Earning.

CHAPTER 31:
37 Ways That You Can Start Earning

"Wealth is the ability to experience life fully." – Henry David Thoreau

Every successful business has one thing in common.

Do you know what it is?

Let me tell you.

Every successful business provides a solution to a problem.

As you get older, you will discover a great universal truth to life.

And that is that how much money we make - is directly proportional to how much value we bring.

So, if you want to make more money, you need to become more valuable.

Makes sense, right?

So rather than starting a business by thinking 'How much money can I make?' - change your thinking.

And instead, go into a business asking 'How can I really help?'

How can I serve? What are people's struggles? What problems can I solve?

As soon as you start to think like this, everything changes.

And so, with that said, let's jump into 37 ideas for businesses that you could create, that can solve people's problems.

At the end of these 37, we will pick a handful and dig deeper into the exact steps for how you can set them up and grow and scale them.

And by the way, you can find more details at any time about these businesses, at our website: http://funancialfreedom.com

37 WAYS THAT YOU CAN START EARNING

1: Driveway Sweeping

Seriously!

Super simple, solves a real problem and can make you a lot of money.

Show up and someone's door and rap "We are the sweeping driveway team. We'll sweep your driveway nice and clean".

It will work like a charm!

2: Social Media Manager

As a teenager, if you have a good understanding of various social media platforms, you can start earning income by managing the social media accounts of local businesses who often have no idea of what they are doing.

If you can help grow followers, get fans, create stories, anything really to increase the reach of a local business, you become a very valuable asset.

Growing up in the Internet age, you have a terrific advantage over many adults.

Companies pay good money for those with expertise in managing YouTube, Instagram etc., and there are plenty of teens and who earn good coin as social media managers.

3: Babysitter

All you need is an excellent reputation or great references, and the ability to find local parents.

There are lots of sites like Care.com and Sittercity.com that allow you to put up a profile to find local jobs.

Babysitting is a great way to earn money because there are almost no start-up costs.

4: Computer Tutor:

Chances are, you are pretty hot with a computer or laptop.

You know how to organize files, troubleshoot, set up email, etc.

Not everyone possesses these skills, particularly older adults.

Therefore, you have the opportunity to impart your knowledge, teaching someone how their computer works, how to navigate the Web, how to set up a cloud account, how to share photos with their grandkids etc.

Or you can focus more on teaching clients how to set up their new devices and/or solve other tech issues.

5: Sell Your (Old) Clothes Online

This is perfect for you if you want to be run a stress-free business entirely from your phone.

There is a fantastic app called Mercari that allows you to sell pretty much anything you want, direct from your phone, and it could not be easier to use.

Teenagers are already making between a few hundred to a few thousand dollars, selling mainly their clothes that either they have grown out of or they just don't want.

But it's not just clothes that you can sell, you can sell pretty much anything, electronics, jewellery, console games, etc.

Once Mercari is on your phone, there are just 3 steps to earning.

Step 1: Snap a photo of what you want to sell, add a description, add a price, and upload your pic.

Step 2: Your item will them appear on Mercari. More often than not someone will buy it within a few days.

Step 3: As soon as your item sells, Mercari will email you a pre-paid postage label. All you do is print this out, slap it on an envelope, and mail the item to your buyer. That's it.

1 - 2 - 3.

A Mercari Online Selling Business is a very enjoyable and straightforward business that can run entirely from your phone.

> DEEPER DIVE: This is one of the Business's that we will do a DEEPER DIVE into in the next chapter.

6: Errand Runner

A smart way to earn money to look at what there is a demand for.

And recently, sites such as TaskRabbit and Handy have boomed in popularity.

These are sites where people can hire people to do errands for them, from picking up dry cleaning, to shopping services, hanging pictures, pretty much everything.

The one thing that everyone wants more of (apart from money) is TIME.

Errands take up a lot of people's time, so a business or service that solves this problem is an excellent way for you to earn.

7: YouTube Personality

This is a fascinating business that has exploded in the last few years.

YouTube allows everyone to create their own channel, for free.

How about creating video content for your own channel?

You can make the videos directly from your phone, and film them anywhere. Your bedroom, garage, out and about.

All you need to decide is what it is you would talk about.

Maybe it could be a review channel — perhaps you review video games, or makeup, or what celebrities are up to.

Or maybe you have a particular theme of something you are interested in, being an entrepreneur, traveling, a specific TV show or band or sports team.

A popular video can go viral generating you an unlimited amount of views for that video and new subscribers for your channel.

There are many ways to earn using YouTube, from allowing ads to show on your videos, to getting sponsorship for each video you make, to even being paid to mention a product or service in your videos.

8: Start a Podcast

If you prefer to talk rather than be seen on video, have you thought about having your own podcast?

Again, you can have a podcast on whatever topic you like.

The key, however, is to be consistent. Many people start a podcast and never record more than one episode.

Our advice would be - choose what you would like your podcast to be about - and record 6 episodes in advance before you go live - to give you some momentum.

And each episode does not have to be crazy long.

If your content is compelling, it's okay to have episodes less than 10 minutes.

There are apps such as anchor.fm that allow you to record into your phone, and then with one click, upload your podcast to all the popular directories (such as iTunes and Google Play).

Advertisers are lining up to pay podcasters sponsorship money.

9: Patreon

Patreon is an incredible service you should be aware of if you are creative.

If you create music, or if you're a designer or writer, or if you sing, or direct, or anything in the artistic field, did you know you can earn money to create what you love!

Patreon.com allows people to discover what it is you do - and then if they like it - they will pay you a small amount of their choice in exchange for exclusive experiences.

For example, if you create YouTube Videos, you could offer an exclusive opportunity for your Patreon Fans.

In return for a small payment (that your fans choose), you will mention their names personally at the end of your videos. Or have the names scrolling at the end, like at the end of a movie.

You would not believe how people are MORE than happy to pay for an exclusive experience.

Patreon already has paid out over $350million to its content creators.

10: Sell Crafts on Etsy

Are you arty?

Do you know how to make awesome bracelets?

Can you make jewellery?

Do you make your own soap, or candles, or clothes?

How about artwork? Do you paint? Or sculpt? Or draw?

Maybe you knit or take photographs.

If you enjoy doing anything creative, did you know you can earn by selling your artwork by creating your own 'stall' on Etsy.com

#11: Post-Construction Clean-Up

Ok, granted, this may not sound the most glamorous, but there is money in that dirt!

With your entrepreneurial hat on, look at the amount of construction that is going on in your neighborhood.

And we mean residential construction (i.e. people have work done on their houses) - not commercial construction (which are things like shopping malls, restaurants etc.)

All contractors are supposed to clean up after themselves, but they are notorious for never doing this very well.

Again, remember any successful business, solves a problem.

So, solving the actual problem of cleaning up after less than diligent construction workers, is a problem that many people will pay well for.

#12: Laundry Run

We discussed being an errand runner earlier.

You can even get more specific and offer to do a laundry run for your local clients.

Going to a launderette is chore than many people will pay others to do, so another excellent opportunity for you to earn.

Remember not to wash red socks with the whites!

Plus, you could offer to do a Dry Cleaners run and pick up service too.

13: Graphic Designer

There are loads of people out there who are looking for graphic artists.

If you have some basic design skills, you can start your own design business where you help clients by designing logos, creating images and other branding elements.

There is almost an unlimited supply of people who want images for their blog, their website, their articles etc.

And sites like Fiverr.com allow you to advertise your services directly to an active database of people looking for your skills.

In fact Fiverr.com is a great site for you to know if you have ANY creative skills. We will come back to Fiverr.com later in this chapter.

#14: Garage Sale

A garage sale, or a yard sale as it's also known, is an effortless way to earn a few hundred dollars, by selling things may otherwise have been thrown away.

Garage sales are fun, they don't take too much work, and can be very profitable.

According to the New York Times, if you put some thought and planning into your garage sale, you can net between $500 and $1,000. That's not too bad, is it?

And it's unlikely it will cost you anything to put on.

All you will need are some picnic tables - a cashbox - maybe a full-length mirror if you want to allow customers to try clothes (if you are selling clothes) - and a calculator.

DEEPER DIVE: This is one of the Business's that we will do a DEEPER DIVE into in the next chapter.

#15: Blogging

If you have knowledge of a particular subject matter or field, blogging could be a good way for you to earn.

Essentially all blogging means is creating valuable and educational content and sharing it on your blog.

The more consistent you are, the more popular your blog posts will become.

And you can earn from your blog by having links and images that link to products that people can purchase.

If someone does click through your link and make a purchase, you make a % of that sale.

This is known as Affiliate Marketing, and a lot of bloggers create blogs purely to tap into the power of affiliate marketing.

16: App Development Company

Have you had an idea for an app?

If so - what's to stop you making it happen?

There are lots of apps being sold on app stores, but there is always the demand for more.

A popular strategy is for an app to be free so you can get a lot of users, but have what is known as an 'upsell' within the app.

This is where a user will have to pay a small amount to access a premium service.

Spotify, for example, has a free version, but it comes with adverts after every few songs.

The paid version of Spotify allows the user to have no ads.

A lot of teenagers have mastered computer programming and software design.

Even if you are not skilled at developing apps, it is a skill you can acquire within a short period of time if you are willing to learn.

So, if this sounds like you, brainstorm with some friends for a killer idea that you could either create yourself - or get created (but you keep ownership) that can be used on computers, tablets and smartphones.

If you can come up with a unique app, you will be amazed at how much you can earn.

#17: Moving Assistant

For most people, moving house or office is a very stressful experience.

Remember, the most successful businesses are those that solve a problem.

How about becoming a professional organizer to help assist those struggling with the overwhelm of a move?

All this would take is good organizational skills, and the ability to remain calm under pressure.

This can be a top-rated service to offer, particularly for seniors who find packing and moving to be physically and emotionally demanding.

#18: Web Design

Everyone needs a website.

Many people still think that creating a website is extremely complicated and time-consuming.

It doesn't have to be.

There are now simple services like SquareSpace and Wix, that allow you to create kick ass and killer websites, without having to have any coding skills.

Approach local businesses that may have a dated website and explore if they would be open to having you create a new site for them.

You'll also discover after just a few clients, if you do a good job your clients will be more than happy to refer you to others.

#19: Dog Walking

Pretty self-explanatory this one!

Did you know in the recession in 2008, one of the only industries that were not affected was the pet industry!

People will always look after their pets, often putting them before themselves!

And in these time-poor days that most people live in, having some help around the house is always a welcome relief.

Focus on getting just a few local and regular clients, and you will be earning a regular and recurring income that will slowly increase your bank balance.

20: Become a Virtual Assistant

More and more people are working from home, or working while they travel.

Since 2000, the term Virtual Assistant (VA) has become more and more popular.

A VA is someone who offers a variety of services for their client, but they often live miles away.

Often a VA will be in a different State, maybe a different time zone, or even a different country.

As a VA you will work from your home.

For example, a VA may answer emails for someone, manage their Facebook Messenger messages, organize their Calendar etc.

There is always a great deal of trust between an employer and his/her VA.

Therefore, you have to be trustworthy, and meticulous.

If you like details and are organized, you may want to explore further becoming a VA.

21: Create Custom Apparel

If you love clothes and fashion, did you know there is big business in custom apparel?

This means, creating your own t-shirts, beanies, joggers and any other article of clothing.

Many websites allow you to create personalized clothing, from hats to hoodies and anything in-between.

A great fun business could be personalizing articles of clothing with pictures that your customer wants.

Personalized tee's for someone's birthday, a customized cap for a celebration, you get the general idea.

Your customer provides the artwork, you design it and get it approved, before placing the order.

Selling personalized t-shirts and apparel online has become very popular.

Fun, simple, and an enjoyable way to earn.

22: Creating eBook Covers for Aspiring Authors

More and more people are writing their own books these days.

That's because the barrier to entry is a lot lower.

It used to be extremely difficult to get a book published.

Nowadays, however, you can self-publish on Amazon.

However - that has resulted in an explosive demand for eBook covers.

All authors need to have a cover for their book.

And this is a design skill that most authors don't have.

So, creating an eBook cover can be very profitable.

There are online tools such as MyEcoverMaker that allow you, as the designer, to create an engaging image for authors.

Not only that, but there are many different styles of book design that you can create, from 3d to a spiral bound book cover, to a pamphlet, to lots more.

If working from home creating beautiful and professional eBook covers is something that appeals to you, then you need to investigate this earning opportunity further.

> GUESS WHAT?! DEEPER DIVE: This is one of the Business's that we will do a DEEPER DIVE into in the next chapter.

#23: Housesitting

There is a booming business for trustworthy individuals to house sit while the house owners are away, either on vacation, or business or maybe due to medical reasons.

Many homeowners would prefer to have someone trustworthy either staying in their home while they are away or at least checking in on the house every day.

House sitters are responsible for general upkeep and maintenance of the property — from collecting the mail, watering the plants, feeding the pets, taking in the Amazon delivery etc.

24: Music Lessons

Can you play an instrument?

If so - you have a golden opportunity to teach others.

Even if you have never taught before, you can turn your skill into a business by charging less than more 'established' teachers in your area.

Also, you will find many people are happy to learn from a 'less experienced teacher' particular as it is costing them less.

You can even do virtual lessons now over Skype, and you can record them and sell the recordings too!

25: Language/Academic Private Tutoring

Similarly to #23 above, do you have a skill that you can offer as private tutoring?

Maybe you are good at math, or Spanish, or geometry, or science.

Offer your services for private 1 on 1 tutoring. Either someone comes to your house, or you charge a bit more, and you travel to theirs.

You can even do virtual lessons now over Skype, and you can record them and sell the recordings too!

26: Create an Online Training Product

If you have a particular skill set, how about creating an Online Course?

Unlike #24 above, you are not swapping your time for money if you have something online.

After a bit of hard work to create it, you can almost 'set and forget' it.

There are many sites such as Udemy and Linda.com that allow you to sell your courses on their platform (and they take a % of each sale)

Or you can use your own platform, such as Teachable or Thinkific.com - and keep 100% of all sales that you generate.

#27: Mobile Car Wash

So, if you want to earn an extra $50 to $200 this weekend (and every weekend) - consider this.

How about creating a mobile car wash - that can benefit your neighbors - or indeed for anybody that is walking distance from your house.

Many successful businessmen and women have started their entrepreneurial journey with their own Car Wash.

The great thing about this business is it is straightforward to set up - while at the same time being very helpful for your neighbors - who often don't have to drive to a car wash and wait in line to get their car cleaned. So - it's a real win-win.

The reason that many people would be interested in your service is because it provides a personalized service right at their home.

GUESS WHAT?! DEEPER DIVE: This is one of the Business's that we will do a DEEPER DIVE into in the next chapter.

28: Gift Baskets

Here's a simple business idea that you can tie in with school breaks.

Creating a Gift Basket.

Gift Baskets can be extremely varied, which makes this a great fun opportunity to allow you to flex your creative muscles.

For a fixed fee, you will sell a gift basket full of goodies.

You will naturally have to factor in the price of obtaining the goodies and the basket into the cost of your Gift Baskets.

But taking orders from friends of your family and your neighbors can be a good earner for you.

For example, could you create Easter Gift Baskets? Maybe you sell each one for $30, yet it only costs you $14 to get a basket, get some tissue paper to make it presentable, and you source some contents, goodies and chocolates, to make the basket a wonderful gift.

Designing gift baskets is a great way to express your creative side.

And this business comes with natural busy seasons (Easter, Mother's Day, Christmas, Thanksgiving, Halloween). Bonus!

29: Party Entertainer

Do you have a skill you can use to entertain others?

Are you good at magic tricks? Can you tell jokes well? Can you twist and turn balloons?

If you have the personality to match, you can earn as an entertainer at special events.

Maybe you can tell kids stories in different voices. Or you can do impressions. Or you're a great mime artist.

Entertaining at events with a particular skill that you have could be an earning opportunity that you may not have investigated until now.

30: Musician

Just like #29 above, if you are musically talented, you could hire out your services for special events.

Playing the piano at a dinner party, or guitar at a BBQ.

Or entertaining guests while they arrive at a birthday or anniversary dinner.

31: Holiday Decorator

This is undoubtedly seasonal, but during the holidays you can offer a service to put up Christmas lights and other decorations.

A lot of older residents would be interested in this.

And there is the perfect opportunity to 'upsell' an additional service to remove the lights and decorations, once the festive period is over.

32: Event and Portrait Photographer

If you enjoy taking photos, this next idea is almost a no-brainer.

How about becoming a photographer?

The only thing you would need a professional camera (so not your cell phone camera) and a good, positive character and personality.

We are living in an age where a picture tells a thousand words.

As a result, there is a massive demand for Event Photographers, and Portrait Photographers, and Family Photographers.

Or you may find you particularly enjoy taking pictures of pets, or children. Or babies.

How about your school? Could you speak to a principal about being your School Photographer?

Again, once we start thinking like an entrepreneur, it's amazing the opportunities that can unfold for us.

If you have a drone, you will have even more amazing opportunities!

#33: Teach a Class at Your Home

If you have a particular skill for something, how about organizing a class in your home to share your talent with local neighborhood teens.

For example, you may be great at street dance, or drawing, or painting.

Your class could be a one-off, or it could run for a weekend, or maybe a few days during school vacation.

Naturally, you'll want to clear this with your parents, and you should pay them a small something for the use of the house.

But teaching a class to friends and locals, who are interested in knowing more about your particular skill, is a fun and fast way to make some extra money.

#34: Use Fiverr To Showcase Your Creative Skills

Do you have a particular creative skill?

For example, are you good at drawing cartoons? Or caricatures? Can you design business logos? Do you know how to edit videos, do voice-overs, design web pages?

If so, you should explore using Fiverr to earn some extra cash.

Fiverr.com provides a platform for individuals to offer their creative services to customers worldwide. Over three million services are listed on Fiverr.

And Fiverr is easy to use. It's free, you create a profile that shows off the creative skill you have, and then your talent is available for all to see.

35: Stock Photographer

If you enjoy looking at the world and people through a creative eye, this could be for you.

Did you also know, some websites will buy your photos from you.

This is known as providing 'stock photography.'

There are a bazillion websites, and blogs, and magazines, and articles and online content, that need images.

A lot of these content creators will purchase images from Stock Photography websites, such as Shutterstock, Fotolia and iStockphoto.com.

Most stock photography sites will accept submissions.

So, if you have a particular look and feel to your pictures (they won't be interested in views of sunsets and mountains), then you can earn money from pictures that are already clogging up your camera roll on your phone.

Upload a selection of your best photos to these Stock Photography sites to gauge the interest.

36: De-Cluttering Service

I don't know about you, but I always feel so much better when I have decluttered my closet or my garage!

And you know what, most people feel the same, but most people never get around to doing this.

So here we have another opportunity to solve a problem!

How about offering a de-cluttering service?

All this really means is organizing someone's closet. Or it could be their garage or shed.

Often people are happy for you to take things from their garage they don't want (obvs ask their permission first), and you could then sell these items at a Garage Sale (see #14)

Your customers will feel better and more organized as a result of your de-cluttering service, and will no doubt tell some friends about you.

37: Cleaning Service

If you enjoy keeping things neat and tidy, how about providing a Cleaning Service?

This could be a service that assists with tidying up and cleaning inside houses.

Or for an additional cost, you could offer services such as cleaning out window wells, clean out gutters, wash trash cans, wash patios and porches etc.

And you could also offer a yard cleanup service, where you trim bushes, pick up poop, pull weeds. Get an extension brush and sweep down wasp nests and spider webs etc. You get the general idea.

Particularly for an older generation, this is a much in demand service that can earn you good money, and regular income too.

Maybe you offer an upsell (i.e. you charge extra) to dispose of trash that your customers no longer want.

SUMMING UP!

- So - there we go - 37 ideas of how you can get started to EARN.

- It's never too early to start thinking like an entrepreneur.

- At the very least, we hope these ideas have lit a fire under you that you can indeed start earning an income of your own, often for minimal effort.

- Obviously, we are not expecting you to create every business we have listed here!

- All we would suggest is ask yourself which one (or two) excites you the most, which one could you see yourself doing, which one feels fun and has got your creative juices going? Then, that's the one to explore further.

- The key is, as we discussed way back in Chapter 1, to take action.

- Don't forget - you can find out more about all of these businesses at any time — by visiting our website: http://funancialfreedom.com

CHAPTER 32:
Deeper Dive –
Introduction

What we are wanting to do in this section is to get you excited at what you can achieve.

Let's light that entrepreneurial fire inside you.

We know you have the potential to be limitless.

To achieve more than you ever thought possible.

But most people go through life with the handbrake on.

Did you know, less than 1% of people fulfill their potential.

In fact, statisticians have even put a number to it:

0.9%.

0.9% of people – so they say – fulfill their potential.

0.9 %! That's all!

However - 0.9% of the world's population is still about 67 million people.

So, the question is, are you going to be one of these 67 million?

Woody Allen said it best "...the world is run by people who show up. When you talk to any successful person, they all say that in life, there are either results or excuses."

Results or excuses.

Which are you going to choose?

I suspect it's results.

So, with that in mind, let's take a deeper dive and get more detailed in some of the business ideas we have shared with you.

We have handpicked at random 4 of the businesses - to go into more detail with.

You may like to know, you can experience more information on all of these business ideas - at our website http://funancialfreedom.com.

The 4 businesses we have decided to do a deeper dive into are:

- Selling your (old) clothes online
- Hosting a garage sale
- Creating eBook Covers for Aspiring Authors
- Mobile Car Wash

CHAPTER 33:
Deeper Dive 1 – Selling Your (Old) Clothes Online

How to create an online selling empire entirely from your phone.

In this first deeper dive - let's explore further this fantastic EARNING opportunity that you have, with something that you already have in your pocket.

Your cell phone.

We think you are going to love this.

Just before we jump in - let us tell you about our PLAYBOOKS.

We have created for you your very own 'cheat sheet' that breaks down exactly how all these businesses work.

We are calling these our PLAYBOOKS - and you can download for free a PLAYBOOK for this business by visiting our site at http://funancialfreedom.com.

So back to this EARNING idea.

We are really pumped to share with you an incredible business that is just beginning to blow up in popularity.

As a result, more and more teenage entrepreneurs are getting involved.

This is perfect for you if you want to run a stress-free business entirely from your phone.

Yes, you heard that correctly - this business is run entirely from your phone.

There is a fantastic app called Mercari that allows you to sell pretty much anything you want, direct from your phone, and it could not be easier to use.

And get this - teenagers are already making between a few hundred to a few thousand dollars, selling mainly their clothes that either they have grown out of or they just don't want.

But it's not just clothes that you can sell, you can sell pretty much anything, electronics, jewellery, console games, etc.

This is a perfect business to run from home, it's slick, simple, and it's fun.

So, if this is something that you like the sound of, let's take more of a look at how you can set up your own Online Selling Business and run it all through your mobile phone.

How This Business Works

So Mercari is very easy to use.

The first thing you have to do is download the app to your phone or tablet.

Once it's installed - create your free account. Then - there are just 3 simple steps to selling.

Step 1: Snap a photo of what you want to sell, add a description, add a price, and upload your pic.

Step 2: Your item will them appear on Mercari. More often than not someone will buy it within a few days.

Step 3: As soon as your item sells, Mercari will email you a pre-paid postage label. All you do is print this out, slap it on an envelope, and mail the item to your buyer. That's it. As soon as the item is received by the buyer, you get paid.

1 - 2 - 3.

Selling Your First Item

Now you understand how Mercari works - all you have to do is get started.

So, have a think.

To start off with - test just one thing. What have you got that you no longer need, or no longer use?

What clothes do you no longer wear?

What gadgets do you no longer use?

What do your parents/brother/sister no longer need? (ask them first!)

Find your first item to sell - just to get comfortable with how Mercari works.

Once you take a picture of the item, you'll then be asked to give a description.

Be as descriptive and as accurate as you can be, as buyers rate you - and you want to get a 5-star rating.

You can also add hashtags so buyers can search for items that match the hashtags you add.

As soon as your item is on Mercari, it is ready to be sold.

Many items sell very quickly, within a day or two, so be prepared for a quick sale.

Let's quickly turn our attention to shipping.

When you list an item, you get to choose who pays for the shipping.

Either you can pay, meaning you'll make a bit less, or the buyer can pay, meaning the buyer will have the shipping added to the sale price.

You may like to know that any item that has shipping included usually sells a bit quicker - that said - if someone wants your item it's highly likely they'll also be fine with paying the shipping.

I'd suggest to start off with - you select 'buyer pays shipping.'

Now, Mercari make their money by taking a flat 10% of the sale price.

So, they get 10%, you get 90%. Simple.

As soon as you make a sale, Mercari will email you a prepaid shipping label.

All you have to do is package the item, put the prepaid label on it, and mail it.

You get paid as soon as your buyer receives your item, so it makes sense to ship it as soon as you can.

And that's it!

Lots of teenagers are making a serious profit by selling unused stuff laying around their home!

Now it's your turn!

A Few Things to Note:

Here are a few tips to make your Mercari Online Selling Business even more enjoyable.

Tip 1: Be organized! Have packing supplies ready. Once you make a sale, you should ship your item within 3 business days of purchase.

Tip 2: Package the item carefully and use bubble wrap for all fragile items. If you are selling clothes, we recommend purchasing some Poly Mailers. Poly Mailers are lightweight, protective envelopes. If you have bought clothes online before, it's likely they turned up in a Poly Mailer. We suggest putting the article of clothing you are selling maybe firstly in some tissue paper, just so it looks more presentable, and then putting it all in a Poly Mailer.

Tip 3: Consider including a thank you note for the buyer. Personal touches can turn a one-time sale into a repeat customer.

Just these 3 simple tips can make your online selling business as efficient as possible.

Time to Get Started!

This EARN opportunity makes it super easy - and super fun - to sell anything online.

Our advice would be - give it a go.

But be warned - it can become addictive!

But being an entrepreneur is.

And as soon as you see income coming in from your efforts, you will want to do more.

Many Mercari sellers do the following.

They go through their closet every few months, take out everything they want to get rid of, and then snap a photo of each item.

They then add the descriptions and hashtags and of course the price.

And finally, they click one button to upload the photo. That's it.

As soon as you make a sale all you have to do is print the label, put in it the Poly Mailer, and take it to the Post Office.

You can spend less than an hour a week with your Mercari business, yet at the same time make some very good money.

Many Mercari sellers are making between a few hundred and a few thousand dollars selling new and used items - and remember - you don't have just to sell clothes.

You can sell pretty much anything with your Mercari Online Store.

Ok - that's it for this first DEEP DIVE.

Let's jump into another!

TO SUM UP: The Key Takeaways from this chapter:

- Mercari is a great app that allows you to sell pretty much anything you want direct from your phone.

- Teenagers are already making between a few hundred to a few thousand dollars, selling mainly their clothes that either they have grown out of or they just don't want.

There are 3 simple steps to using Mercari:

- Step 1: Snap a photo of what you want to sell and upload.

- Step 2: Your item will them appear on Mercari and often sells within a few days.

- Step 3: As soon as you make a sale Mercari will email you a pre-paid postage label. Put this on an envelope and mail the item to your buyer.

CHAPTER 34:
Deeper Dive 2 – Host Your Own Garage/Yard Sales

Let's continue with another Deep Dive into an EARNING opportunity for you.

The key thing with any successful business is to keep it simple.

As we have said before - so many people over-complicate things — there really is no need.

And here is a very simple — but very effective idea to allow you to start EARNING.

Run a garage sale. Or a yard sale as it's also called.

This is a straightforward way to earn a few hundred dollars, by selling things may otherwise have been thrown away.

Yard sales are fun, they don't take too much work, and can be very profitable. So, let's jump into running yours.

Preparing For Your Garage/Yard Sale

First things first - decide upon a date for your yard sale.

Saturdays or Sundays are best - usually around 10 in the morning.

Check the long-range weather forecast to avoid rain ruining your day.

Once you have a date - and we suggest you plan it two weeks out - now is the time to start gathering items to sell.

Ask your family for help - and go through each room in your house, including the basement, the attic, the long-forgotten closet in the guest bedroom, the backyard shed, and anywhere else you might find items that are no longer serving you.

Make sure that you ask permission to sell any item that is not yours - you don't want to cause a family war by selling your sister's cuddly iguana even if she hasn't used it for years.

As you gather your items - it pays to be organized.

Box them up by category - for example, you may have boxes for books, clothes, toys, home decor, kitchenware, tools, etc.

Having your items organized in advance of your sale will make the day itself run more smoothly.

One thing worth mentioning is, you may find it more difficult than you think to let go of some of your stuff.

A lot of us are emotionally attached to things.

A good rule to set yourself is as follows: if you have not used the thing you are thinking of selling for over a year - it goes in the sale.

Be ruthless!

It also feels good to declutter.

You could call in help from relations and friends to also donate any items they no longer need.

Very soon you will have a few boxes in your bedroom over-flowing with goodies for your forthcoming yard sale.

Good work y'all!

How Much Will Your Garage Sale Cost/How Much Can You Make?

So when it comes to how much can you make from your garage sale, there are no national statistics available.

However, according to the New York Times, if you put some thought and planning into your garage sale, you can net between $500 and $1,000.

That's not too bad, is it?

But how much will it cost you to put on?

The good news is - it's likely it won't cost you anything.

All you will need are some picnic tables - a cashbox - maybe a full-length mirror if you want to allow customers to try on any of the clothes - and a calculator.

One thing that is important of course is pricing.

You may be tempted to price every item you put up for sale.

But guess what? You won't make as much money this way!

It's been proven if you don't price your goods you will make more money.

Let me repeat that - do not price your items!

Instead, let the buyer name the price.

If it's not quite what you had in mind, and it's early in the sale, say no.

But often a buyer will love something you don't care much for and may be perfectly willing to give you more than you think it's worth.

Another reason not to price items is it's tedious and time-consuming.

And pricing makes people procrastinate.

So, once you have the date, and some items - and incidentally you want to have at least 100 items to sell, less than that and your yard sale will not look that appealing - now we are ready to promote the big day itself.

Marketing Your Garage Sale

The more people at your sale, the better, so make sure you advertise.

Your advertising can be as creative as you feel.

Design simple posters and attach them to lampposts.

Maybe design a flyer and deliver it to houses around the hood.

You may want to call some local kids together to help you with this.

Visit neighbors and invite them to join the event.

People are much more inclined to make the trek to a busy street sale.

A few days before your Yard Sale you may want to consider advertising online.

Craigslist is still the most widely used website for yard sale listings, and it is free.

You may also consider checking out yardsalesearch.com or see if you can find a local Facebook group that advertises yard sales.

Mention it on your own personal social media channels too.

Newspaper classified ads will generally charge a fee, and not nearly as many people these days read newspapers - so I would stay away from this.

Think about using public bulletin boards, too.

Most Starbucks have a bulletin board where they allow local businesses to put up a flyer.

Do you have other coffee shops near to you that do the same?

You could ask your church if they have a bulletin board - or maybe if you give them enough notice - they may have a newsletter they send out to their parishioners in which they could include information about your sale.

Any messaging needs to be simple and clear, merely say YARD SALE, and include the date, address and time.

The marketing for any business is always the most crucial part.

Most people get overexcited about an idea - but an idea alone is worthless.

You have to take action on your idea - this is what all millionaires understand, and all millionaires do.

The Day Itself

Entrepreneurs learn at an early age that building a fulfilling and prosperous life for themselves begins by creating their own business.

So well done on putting in some sweat equity to create your own yard sale.

Now the day itself is here.

Aim to be all set up 30 minutes before you begin.

You also need time to make the items presentable.

If practical, set up separate tables for books, sporting goods and garden tools, and organize clothing by size, maybe on a rail if you have one.

Have your cashbox handy with lots of change.

And then if you have told your neighbors and conducted a bit of advertising, visitors will begin to arrive.

It's natural to feel a bit nervous at first, but the most important thing of all is to enjoy yourself ☺

Have fun.

You may want to consider having an 'upsell' at your garage sale too.

An upsell is an opportunity for you to earn some extra money, but offering a different but related service.

So, think about what upsells you could have at your yard sale.

For example, could a friend or brother or sister - sell drinks?

Just a cup of lemonade, or maybe coffee for the adults, could easily make you 50 cents or $1 per cup.

Sell 50 of those over the course of the yard sale, and that's a significant extra amount of money you have made purely from your upsell.

Allow yourself to have fun when thinking about upsells - no idea is too stupid.

Maybe you have a friend that is good at drawing caricatures.

Could he/she charge $5 per caricature and you split the profits 50/50?

Imagine offering lemonade and caricatures at your yard sale!

Your dollar value of your customer is going to increase, as you have more products to offer.

Once you start thinking like this — as an entrepreneur - the possibilities are endless.

This is why having your own business is so much fun — you get to make the rules….

When it's time to close up shop, the last thing you want to do is bring the unsold items back into your home.

Although we advise not to price what you are selling, as your day draws to a close there is nothing wrong with creating a sign such as 'Everything on this table is $1.00' to get rid of much as possible.

Anything that is not sold you may want to take to a local charity that will accept the types of items you are selling.

In the US there are Goodwill Centers everywhere that accept a broad range of items.

You could easily drop your unsold items off at a Goodwill Center at the end of the day, leaving you with just a pile of cash from your sales.

As you get the knack of running garage sales, you will discover this is an exciting way to start to earn and run your own business.

A Few Other Things You Should Know About Garage Sales

In no particular order, I want to share with you a few other things that you should know.

1. Depending on local laws, it's possible, although unlikely, that a permit may be needed for a garage sale. Some areas may restrict or ban the posting of fliers on telephone poles/signposts. If you're uncertain about local regulations, check with the mayor's office or the town hall.

2. Don't be embarrassed about selling items that you think are silly, broken or utterly without value. Remember, the general rule is if no one's used the item in the last year, then after getting permission, include it in the sale. There is a saying in the selling world that one man's trash is another man's treasure.

3. You may want to provide a mirror for trying on clothing, and maybe an extension cord so shoppers can test appliances.

4. As we have mentioned, Saturdays are the best day for your yard sale, but be cautious of holiday weekends.

Also, whereas naturally, we don't want rain, believe it or not, we also don't want it to be too sunny!   Sunny skies are often overrated to make sales in because on a beautiful day, people will be off doing other things. The perfect weather would be clouds!

TO SUM UP: The Key Takeaways from this chapter:

*   Garage sales are a fun and a simple way to start earning.

*   There are probably enough items around your house that aren't being used to have regularly scheduled weekend garage sales.

*   Flex your entrepreneurial muscles even more and ask yourself could you find items and deals at local thrift stores, or 99 cent stores, or even other garage sales, to sell at yours?

CHAPTER 35:
Deeper Dive 3 – Creating eBook Covers for Aspiring Authors

If you'd like a Deep Dive into another business that you can run from the privacy of your bedroom and your computer - then this is for you.

In the early 2000's when the internet was really beginning to get popular, if you offered any service in that industry such as making websites for people - you would have done very well.

When social media began around 2006, anyone that created information products about any of the social media platforms again did very well.

Computer games are booming now - look at how many YouTube personalities there are that essentially just play games while filming themselves. These influencers are making millions — all because they saw a trend and they positioned themselves in front of it.

Selling personalized t-shirts and apparel online has become very popular.

In the last few years, anything to do with Cryptocurrency always gets a lot of interest.

Fidget spinners had 12 months of everyone collecting them.

You get the general idea!

The reason we are mentioning this is because a key component of you becoming financially intelligent, is to train your brain to always be on the lookout for what is growing in popularity.

What are your friends talking about?

What is the latest craze at school?

What's everyone watching online?

And this brings us nicely onto this Deeper Dive.

Let us share with you a trend that has only just begun to boom - and a trend that can very quickly make you some money if you position yourself in front of it.

More and more people want to write their own book.

But what used to put people off - was how difficult it used to be to get a book published.

It used to be the only way to publish a book - was you'd have to get an agent who would get you a book deal - and then you'd have to rely on them to get your physical book out into bookstores across the world.

As you can imagine - a hugely challenging and time-consuming endeavor - not to mention super expensive.

However - the good news - is that everything has now changed.

Now - authors no longer need to rely on a publisher - because these days its very easy to self-publish.

Authors can still produce a physical version of their book if they like - but a lot of authors now just publish a digital version - that can be easily downloaded online.

This has made it SO much easier for anyone to publish their book.

And the most prominent online marketplace for authors to publish their book - is of course - Amazon.

Thanks to Amazon and their global dominance - the barrier to publishing a book has now been significantly lowered.

And so - how can we benefit from this?

Well, all these authors have one need in common.

Sure, they have all written a book - but none of them will have a cover for their book.

Yet.

And that's where you come in.

How about setting up an online business creating eBook Covers for this huge demand.

If this appeals to you — and if you would like your business to be 100% online - then creating your own eBook Covers business - is an idea that you should explore.

How an eCover Business Works

So now we know there is a demand for eBook covers.

So, let's explore further if this business is for you.

Essentially there are just 2 steps.

Step 1 - creating the eBook cover

Step 2 - marketing your eBook cover business

In this chapter - let's go through how to create your eBook cover.

The good news is - this is not only very simple - but also a lot of fun.

Let us introduce you to a free tool that will allow you to create epic eBook covers.

It's called MyEcoverMaker.com.

Thanks to MyEcoverMaker it's easy to create beautiful and professional eBook covers — even if you've never designed anything in your life.

We can start from scratch - or we can use one of their professional pre-designed templates and personalize it.

We can create 2D or 3D covers - depending on what your customer wants.

Now MyEcoverMaker offers a free plan - so this is good for you to get started to see if this is something that you really enjoy.

Once you start making some regular money - we would suggest upgrading to the paid plans - that vary between $14 - $22/month. The paid plans have more of pre-created templates - but we can still make impressive eBook covers using the free plan.

How to Make More Money With Your Ebook Cover

So, once we have our eBook Cover - lets now talk about how you can make more money with it.

We can achieve this by offering an upsell.

Most businesses offer some sort of additional service at the point of sale.

In most stores when somebody goes to pay for something - often an additional service is offered.

This is known as an upsell.

You need to know the importance of having upsells.

If somebody is going to purchase your eCover anyway - this is the perfect opportunity to offer them something else (so long as it is related).

So, what could be a great upsell? Well - let's think about this.

If somebody has bought an eBook cover - they may also be interested in having an image of their ebook on a computer monitor.

Or maybe on a mobile phone.

This will give your Customer more images that they can use for their marketing.

The great thing about MyEcoverMaker is that it offers a whole suite of options that we can add the image that you have already created, too.

So how about offering a suite of 5 different images - for $20. That would be a great upsell.

Getting Customers

Ok - so now you have got a little bit familiar with MyEcoverMaker.

Now - it's time to go and get you some paying customers.

And there is one site in particular where people go to get help with their projects like eBook covers.

That site is Fiverr.com.

Fiverr is the world's largest marketplace for digital services.

Now - don't be put off by the name.

Back when fiver started, everything was just, as the name suggests, $5. Now, however, although the name has stayed, you can charge whatever you like for your service.

However, it's generally considered good business to start at $5.

So maybe start by charging $5 for one eBook cover.

However - if you offer a suite of maybe 5 images like we suggested earlier - we'd recommend charging $20 for that.

Once you have the original eBook cover created - and that should take you no more than 20 minutes once you are up to speed with MyEcoverMaker - you can very easily include your upsells for maybe 10 or 15 minutes extra work.

So, if a Customer wanted an eBook cover and an upsell of the suite of images - you should easily be able to create all of these within an hour - and charge $25 or so.

Fiver is a fantastic website.

It allows you to share your talent with the world and get paid for it.

As a slight aside - although we are talking about Fiverr here to sell your eCover Business - you can also use Fiverr to promote any other skill you have, for example, you may be an excellent graphic designer - or great on Photoshop - or a programmer - or translator - voice-over artist - content writer etc. Whatever your talent is - Fiverr allows you to share it with a huge community of buyers.

Getting Started With Your eCover Business.

If you take the time to learn a skill, such as how to create engaging and eye-popping eBook covers - you will always have customers requesting your service.

There is a saying in business that goes 'we get paid for how much value we bring to the marketplace'.

And that is 100% true.

So, if you want to make more money, all you have to do is become more valuable.

Learning a new skill - such as how to create beautiful eBook Covers - is a skill that will make you more valuable.

So, all you need to do now - is get used to creating eBook covers.

Build up your confidence by experimenting with the other designs and templates available.

And then - create your free account at Fiverr and start to advertise your gig.

TO SUM UP: The Key Takeaways from this chapter:

- More and more authors are self-publishing their books online, meaning there is a huge demand for eBook covers.

- There are free (and paid) tools available that allow you to create eBook covers.

- These tools come with pre-created templates that you can customize and personalize to fit with your customer's desire.

CHAPTER 36:
Deeper Dive 4 – Mobile Car Wash

Ok, let's explore another Deep Dive.

All successful businesses have one thing in common - and that is they solve a problem.

And the best businesses are based on a very simple idea.

Here is one of the simplest that you could have up and running by the weekend - and be in profit immediately.

So, if you want to earn an extra $50 to $200 this weekend (and every weekend) - consider this.

How about creating a mobile car wash - that can benefit your neighbors - or indeed for anybody that is within walking distance from your house.

Many successful entrepreneurs have built up their bank account by starting their own Car Wash.

The great thing about this business is it is extremely easy to set up - while at the same time being very helpful for your neighbors - who don't have to drive to a car wash and wait in line to get their car cleaned.

So - it's a real win-win.

The reason that many people would be interested in your service is because it provides a personalized service right at their home.

So - how does it work, how can you set this up, how much can you make and how do you get customers?

Let's dig in and take a look:

Preparing For Your Mobile Car Wash Business

The beauty of this business is you do not need any office or workspace of your own to operate. All of your business will be conducted on your customer's driveways.

Car wash prices vary, but I'd suggest offering a standard outer wash for $10.

Larger vehicles may warrant a few more dollars, I'd suggest $15.

However - you can make a lot more by offering extras.

I'm sure you have noticed that most businesses offer some sort of additional service at the point of sale.

We have talked about this a few times already — these additional services are known as upsells.

So, for example, when you are at McDonalds and they ask 'do you want fries with that?' - that is an upsell"

When you are at a restaurant, and the server asks 'would you like a side salad?' that is an upsell.

Adding one or two upsells to your business is one of the simplest ways to increase your income - so long as the upsell is related to what your customer is purchasing.

So, in your Car Wash business - how could you do this?

Well - how about offering to wax your customer's car after it's been washed - for an additional $10.

Great upsell - it is related to your main offer - the washing of your car - yet you offer it as an extra stand-alone service.

You will be amazed at how many customers will take you up on an upsell - and then from this one simple offer you have doubled your profit. Cool huh!

Or you could offer to clean the inside on the car for an extra $10.

Both very simple upsells. Or you could bundle both upsells together for $15.

Just having a handful of upsells you can offer will make a REAL difference to how much you can make.

Talking of money - let's look at how much your Car Wash business will cost to set up - and how much it could realistically make.

How Much Will it Cost/How Much Can You Make?

Having your own Car Wash Business is a great way to start a simple business with virtually no costs.

All you will need is a few buckets, some sponges and cloths.

That should cost you no more than $20.

The earning potential is enormous.

Just 5 cars washed over a weekend - could earn you $100 if you had a few upsells thrown in.

The potential to earn income is only limited by your time.

Getting the word out about your business and following up with potential customers is going to determine whether your business will succeed or not.

So, if you feel excited that your first step to being financially smart starts by creating your own Mobile Car Wash Business - let's discuss how to get those all important customers.

Marketing Your Car Wash Business

If you run your Car Wash Business correctly - you will not need that many NEW customers all the time - as you will discover a lot of your customers will become REPEAT customers.

This increases the Lifetime Value of your Customer.

In most Businesses, the Lifetime Value of a Customer is the most important number - or metric to give it it's proper term - that business owners need to know.

For now though — you have precisely a big phat zero customers!

We need to change that!

The great news is - you do NOT need many customers to make some good money.

You could easily make $100 a day with just 5 (or less) customers.

But how do we even get these first 5?

I'm glad you asked!

We are going to do this the old-fashioned way.

I would recommend on a Thursday or Friday evening before you intend to start your business, to go door-to-door (with a parent) and introduce yourself to your neighbors and offer your new and exciting business that is starting and is having it's Grand Opening this very weekend!

Maybe you could even have created a simple flyer on your computer and printed it out.

Give your business a creative, fun name and explain what you are doing.

You are aiming to get 5 firm 'YES' commitments from individuals.

That's all.

5 cars should earn you $100+.

Here's a tip for you!

Before you visit any of your neighbors — write out and learn a couple of selling points about your business.

For example - you may say that a major selling point for your car wash is that you offer greater attention to detail than an automatic car wash.

It may take you and your mom/dad/guardian knocking on 15 - 20 doors, that's all, to get your 5 YES's.

Particularly if you know some of your neighbors already.

So, it won't take that long.

Once you have your 5 'YES's' - you have your first 5 customers.

Arrange a time to be at your neighbor's property - and then you are in business!

Remember - this does not have to be complicated!

A business should be simple - it's people that over complicate things.

Arrive on time with your tools - which will most likely be: soap, a bucket, and sponges and rags.

Remind your customer of the price and then offer them any of your upsells.

They may say yes - they may say no!

Deliver your service - and upon completion invite your customer to inspect their vehicle.

If they haven't purchased one of your upsells - here is another perfect time to pitch it.

Don't be afraid to say "Would you like it waxed for just $10?"

Again - you'll be amazed how much extra money you can make at the point of purchase.

Remember - people like to do business with people that they like.

And although you are young - you can still leave a killer impression.

In fact - you can very easily leave a better impression than most adults.

Arrive on time - be polite - do a great job - and it's highly likely this customer will become a REPEAT customer.

Secret Tip to Growing Your Business.

I hope you are beginning to see that starting a profitable business does not have to be complicated.

As a side note - let me share with you a secret that most business owners don't learn until after a few years.

This tip is going to save you a lot of time and give you a head start.

Smart business owners know that the real way to grow a business quickly is to look after their EXISTING customers - and allow them to do the marketing for you.

So, in this example - when you do a great job - your customer may recommend your services to a friend of theirs.

This is the best marketing of all — word of mouth.

This is the only marketing that you cannot buy — and it is the most powerful of all.

So really go far and beyond as much as you can.

Really over deliver.

Maybe you buy a stack of air freshness and leave one in the vehicle as an unadvertised gift.

Maybe you buy some mints and leave a pack with a quick note thanking your customer for his business, on their dashboard.

Anything that can WOW your customer is going to do two things.

Firstly, it's highly likely they will use your business again, so you don't need to find new customers continually — and secondly, it's highly likely they will recommend you to a friend of theirs — again meaning you don't have to go and find new customers continually.

It's interesting - most businesses do the bare minimum to fulfil their promise — yet once you start to think creatively it's SO easy to go way beyond and really over deliver - which will result in you having customers scrambling to use your service and give you money.

Success really comes down to one thing - if you treat people well and allow them to have a great experience - you will have a customer for life.

Test Run

Let us tell you a quick story.

In 2007, two friends in San Francisco had a very simple idea. They decided to test offering their loft as cheap accommodation for travelers coming to town.

They took pictures - put it up on a simple website - and within a few days, they had 3 paying guests. This was how Airbnb started.

The reason we wanted to share this with you - is because before you go visit your customers - it's essential to have a test run.

You will discover many things that you won't have thought about — for example, you may need way more rags than you realize - you may find you want to wear gloves - you may discover that waxing a car takes longer than you thought.

You want to learn things like this while in test mode — rather than on the actual job with a real paying customer.

So, before your big first day - and before you come home with a fistful of dollars - be smart - and have a test run.

There is a great saying in marketing that goes 'a lazy man always does things twice'.

And it's true.

A lazy man will not test - and then will come across a problem on the actual day - and have to do something 2 or 3 times until they get it right.

So - have a test run.

It's fun, it's part of being on the road to being financially free, and it will set you up for success.

TO SUM UP: The Key Takeaways from this chapter:

- The reason that many people would be interested in this service is because it provides a personalized service right at their home.

- This business is very easy to set up while at the same time being very valuable to your neighbors.

- All you need is 5 customers to make $100 or so per weekend

CHAPTER 37:
EARN – Wrapping Up

Hey - check you out.

Here we are, at the end of EARN.

Nice work.

Ok, so now, let's continue with LEAP.

We have educated ourselves in LEARN.

We have explored business ideas in EARN.

Now let's turn our attention to how we can GROW and SCALE our money.

And we will do that next, in ACCELERATE.

SECTION 6: ACCELERATE

CHAPTER 38:
ACCELERATE – Introduction

"If you don't find a way to make money while you sleep, you will work until you die." – *Warren Buffett*

Congratulations on hop, skip and jumping your way through the leap chapters! You are making great time!

Even if its taken you a month or more to get to here you are making great time .... Why?

Well, you are still a teenager, right?

GREAT ... you have lots of time!

That is what this section is all about!

Making your money work for you over time.

In order for this section to make sense, you will need to have read through the learn & earn sections in which we started to tap into your earning potential.

Now it's all about what to do with all that money ... LOL!

Do remember when we spoke about SAVINGS in Chapter 12 here in "I Need Money"?

We talked about breaking out of debt and how scarcity requires MORE than just the ability to earn money.

It also requires the ability to SAVE money.

The rich understand that SAVING is the foundation of wealth.

Remember us discussing this?

The importance of saving cannot be underestimated.

WE MUST SAVE!

Once you start to create any kind of an income, be that from a part-time job, or a business, you have created, or an allowance from your parents, it can be tempting to spend your cash.

However, if you want to make MORE money, then you need to get good at delaying gratification.

That means you need to be disciplined with your money and save some of it.

Sure, you can spend SOME, but not all.

SAVING is cool.

Saving will allow you to accelerate your financial growth.

Saving will allow you to make your money work for you rather than you working for it.

So, let us show you how you can make money while you sleep!

The first step to learning about turning your money into riches is to learn the basics of saving which we have introduced in the LEARN section.

We mentioned the rat race, but now we should explain it a little more.

It basically means that over time no matter how much money we earn in a job, we continue to spend it.

While we think we are getting somewhere, we are actually getting deeper into a trap!

This is what "keeping up with the Joneses" means, where you keep spending more of what you have and take out bad debt to keep up the appearance that everything is all good with money when its only getting worse!

This is why most of the world are either in the debt and scarcity zones is because firstly they don't make enough income, but secondly, they don't know how to hold onto it or SAVE it.

A recent survey from bankrate.com showed that one in four adult Americans do not have a single penny saved while another study found that 64% of Americans don't have $1,000 in cash even to cover an emergency and this is the richest nation in the world!

We MUST save!

The key to saving is to start young and to develop it as a habit.

> **TO SUM UP: The Key Takeaways from this chapter:**
>
> • You are the perfect age to get started saving.
>
> • You need to be saving before you can invest
>
> • The "rat race" is the default place where most people end up in life with their money

CHAPTER 39:
How Do I Save?

"The better you manage your money, the more money you will be given to manage!" – Dr John Demartini

Where do we start?

We are going to make this really easy for you.

We have a very simple system that you can start to use straight away that will set you up an amazing habit that will set you on the path to riches!

The system involves having four separate jars with four different names.

Give.

Save.

Invest.

Spend.

Now please don't laugh (too hard) at this and think that it is childish!

We promise if you start this habit today and continue it into adulthood, you will never have to worry about money again!

Imagine that!

No money worries because of one simple habit!

Yes, that is 100% correct!

This habit is also really good to nail before we get to the stage of opening bank accounts, as we will eventually repeat this exact process with your bank.

So, let's go through how this system works.

There are only 3 steps.

And be warned, it is stupidly simple (the best ideas always are).

STEP 1:

As soon as you receive any money that comes in from any source, we will divide it into four different areas.

To make this simple to manage we recommend getting four see-through plastic money jars.

Or you could use 4 empty coffee jars or something similar at home.

So, that's Step 1 - you need 4 see-through containers.

STEP 2:

Now that we have our four see-through containers, we need to label them.

You will label them as follows:

Give:

Save:

Invest:

Spend:

That's it for Step 2 — all you need to do is name label your containers.

STEP 3:

Ok here's where it gets really exciting!

From now on, ANY time you receive any money, we will divide the money between these 4 jars.

And it doesn't matter where the money comes from: if it's from a part-time job you have, or a side business you have created, or an allowance from your parents, or a Christmas or birthday gift.

ANYTIME you receive ANY money from now on, we will separate it between these 4 jars.

And this is how we will separate it.

The GIVE jar gets 10%

The SAVE jar gets 20%

The INVEST jar gets 20%

The SPEND jar gets 50%

In fact, you may want to write in the container the percentage associated with each.

So, that's Step 3!

Believe it or not, that is the system.

We know it sounds stupidly simple, but the best ideas always are.

Remember when we spoke about Occam's Razor back at the beginning of *I Need Money*?

Whatever is the simplest path - is always the path to take.

So — now that we have our system set up let's go through a real-life example of how it works.

EXAMPLE

Let's take an example that you receive $10, as a gift from your Grandma.

You would split this $10 as follows.

The GIVE jar gets $1

The SAVE jar gets $2

The INVEST jar gets $2

The SPEND jar gets $5

Back in Chapter 6 here in *I Need Money* we talked about how SPECIFIC information is better than generic?

This is precisely what we are doing here.

We are SPECIFICALLY putting aside a percentage of all your income, to Give, Save, Invest and Spend.

You may find this hard to believe, but less than 1% of adults have ANY system to manage their money.

Over 50% of US adults have ZERO savings.

This is the reason why.

They have no system.

If you implement this system and make it a HABIT ANYTIME you get cash in your hands - you will never have financial problems for the rest of your life.

And when you come to open a bank account, we will apply precisely this same 10%/20%/20%/50% split. (Eventually, you will create 4 bank accounts - titled: Give, Save, Invest, and Spend)

Let's now dig down deep and go through EXACTLY what each jar means.

The GIVE Jar

Giving is the first jar that we have as it is a very important concept to understand from an early age.

Firstly, there is a law of the universe.

And that is:

The more you give, the more you receive.

Secondly, there will always be people who are less well off than you are who could do with your help financially to help them.

And thirdly, giving sends a message that your money is abundant and that you are ready to handle more.

A wise mentor of ours once told us, "the better you manage your money, the more money you will be given to manage!"

So, when it comes to the "give" jar, sit down and have a think about if you had spare money that you couldn't spend on yourself or your family or friends, who would you give it to?

What moves you?

What resonates with you?

Who would you really love to be in a position to help?

Would it be a charity that helps children?

When you see homelessness, does a part of you inside want to help them?

Maybe the prevention of cruelty to animals is close to your heart.

How about helping to find a cure or prevention of a disease?

Only you can answer this, and these answers will change as you grow older.

But which part of society would get you EXCITED to help?

You will get in the habit of GIVING 10% of everything you make, to a particular cause that really impacts you.

The SAVE Jar

The SAVE jar is just as it sounds.

The save jar is to be used for things that we would typically save up for.

For example, a computer game, a musical instrument, a pair of sneakers that your parents can't afford for you, going on a foreign school trip etc.

Think about this for a few moments.

What would you love to save for over the next six months?

What have you secretly had your eye on that you would like to own, but you don't yet have the money for it?

Whatever that is, your SAVE jar will slowly allow you to own this item.

And remember, 20% of any income you make, goes into your SAVE Jar.

And you do NOT spend it on anything, except the one thing you are saving for.

The INVEST Jar

Another 20% of any money you make, goes into the INVEST jar.

The invest jar is to be used as our golden goose that lays the golden eggs.

Eventually, the invest jar will be worth more than the other jars combined.

You may remember in EARN we spoke about Compounding Interest.

We are going to come back to Compounding Interest in the next chapter, but we will be using the 20% we put into our INVEST jar to tap into the power of Compounding Interest.

As an extra incentive - you may want to go to Google Images and search for images that inspire you, maybe what your dream house would look like, or a lifestyle image that you aspire too.

You may want to print out an image or two and stick in on your INVEST jar.

Visualizing what it is you would like, helps hugely with keeping focused to achieve it.

The SPEND Jar

Aha! The SPEND jar!

50% of everything you make — you can spend!

Half of all your income - you can spend.

The other half is split between Give, Save and Invest.

The spend jar is to be used for things that we would usually spend money on regularly.

Pizza with friends, Theatre tickets, Shopping at the Mall, those iTunes songs, that app you want, makeup, clothes, snacks, a burrito when you're hungry, bowling, rock climbing......

Anytime you want to purchase anything - you will pay for it from the SPEND jar. If you don't have enough money for your purchase - then you will have to go without until you have more in your SPEND jar.

For all money/income that you receive from now on, divide it out into each of these jars.

You might find that over time you may want to reduce the percentage you put into spend and reallocate it to some of the others.

If you do find yourself with spare money in "spend" ALWAYS move into the "Invest" jar without even hesitating!

This rapidly speeds up your journey to wealth.

> **TO SUM UP: The Key Takeaways from this chapter:**
> - The better you manage your money, the more money you will be given to manage.
> - Give, Save, Invest & Spend are the 4 key cornerstones of a successful saving system
> - Start the habit of saving today and get perfect later

CHAPTER 40:
The JEDI Model

Have you ever wondered what the difference is between the different types of jobs that you can get as an adult?

In school we are trained to study hard to get ourselves a "good" job but what does that really mean?

The problem with this approach is that it misses a very big factor that most people are completely unaware of when selecting their careers.

We are led to believe that getting a "stable" job is the path to riches and a financially abundant future, but the reality is that getting a job very rarely leads to this.

In fact, there really isn't such a thing as a "stable" or "permanent" job anymore.

What we wish to share with you is something called the JEDI model.

This model allows you to wise up to how the system really works and where you should be aiming to be to be financially abundant.

The JEDI model is broken into four separate components.

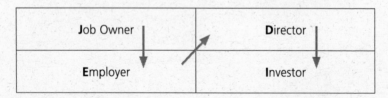

Job Owner	**D**irector
Employer	**I**nvestor

Fig 40.1 The Jedi Model

Job Owner:

The typical starting point for most people on their financial journey is to get themselves a "job" and thereby become a job owner.

The J in Jedi stands for job owner.

This is where you offer your services and skills to somebody else, who will pay you, usually per hour, for the value that you provide to that company.

You can do this from as young as a teenager in most countries, and it tends to be the primary source of peoples' income throughout the world for their entire lives.

On the surface, it seems to be a good option, especially when you are not aware of the other three that exist.

The advantages are that you don't have the risk of owning the business.

You get paid every week or month like clockwork as long as you show up, and your work meets the minimum requirements.

The downsides, however, are large but not often discussed.

Your financial future is now in the hands of someone else.

You can be laid off at any moment and can do nothing about it.

Your job will most likely be moved to a country where the labor is cheaper.

If not, your role could be taken over by automation or computers.

You are paid based on how many hours you work so your earning potential is capped by those hours.

No matter how good of a week you had, you need to return next week and do it all again.

You must work to strict time schedules.

You are probably getting up early at least 5 days a week.

Only a very few people can ever make it to the CEO levels of a company.

You spend most of your time away from the home that you want to be in.

You spend hours in traffic each day going to work in a job that you might not even like.

You are very restricted as to what you can do with your money.

You have very few tax breaks that you can take advantage of.

Any money you spend on vacation is "after-tax" money.

At least 70% of every penny you make goes back to the government in taxes.

You end up living for the weekend!

Your life revolves around planning to have a holiday away from this life.

At a certain point in life, your income source will completely stop when you are no longer "employable".

You are now totally reliant on a pension assuming you have one.

This is normal!

Employer:

The next level in the model is becoming the employer.

The employer most often starts off in a very simple way, where the first person employed is yourself.

This is when you are known as "self-employed".

Quite often though, this person will hire a few more people around them to grow a small business.

The advantages now are that you are in more control of the success of the business.

You get to call the shots.

You don't have to work for anyone else.

You have a lot more options available to you around tax treatment.

You can expense things related directly to the business which was not possible as a job owner.

You have the scope to grow this business to whatever size you wish.

Several downsides come with this too, however.

Usually, the employer works twice as many hours as a regular job owner.

Taking weekends off is a thing of the past.

There is no guarantee that you will even get paid as you generally need to pay everyone else first to make sure they don't leave your business.

There is over a 90% chance that your business if it is a traditional one, is going to fail in the first 5 to 10 years.

Traditional business is very hard work.

You take on all the risks including the financial risks.

You may see your family even less than when you were a job owner.

You run the risk of bankruptcy.

You are probably in a lot of debt and just working to pay back the banks for at least a few years.

You are constantly at the whims of competitors eager to take you out whenever they can.

You no longer get away with being only good at one thing which it was ok to be, as a job owner.

Now you must be good at managing, leading, accounting, sales, marketing, operations, recruitment etc.

You are entering a world of constant stress!

Director:

The third level of the model is making the move from employer to director.

This is where you no longer are involved in the day to day running of the company.

You step out and act in more of a consultation role rather than the highly involved role of the employer.

It usually takes quite a lot of experience and/or coaching and mentoring to make this huge move from stage two (employer) to stage three (director).

It is very possible to be a director in multiple companies allowing you to have a guiding role in many without being tied into the day to day operations of any.

There are many advantages of moving to stage three.

You now can free up your time substantially.

You work on a business rather than in the business.

You are a lot more strategic in your approach so you can spot dangers and opportunities earlier and act earlier.

You usually get paid a lot more than an employer.

You do not have to work to a strict schedule, more so you attend board meetings every now and again.

It allows you to express interests in multiple types of businesses at the same time diversifying your knowledge and growing your experience without having to do the hard graft.

There are some disadvantages too, but not as many as the Job owner or Employer.

You may miss the "hands-on" operations of being more involved.

You don't have as much of a controlling interest in what happens day to day.

Your finances may not be secure yet as you may not be investing at this point in time but it is likely that you are.

Investor:

The fourth stage is the Investor stage.

This is the pinnacle of the model and when you have become a JEDI master!

You now have your money work for you as opposed to you working for money.

You can invest in businesses without ever having to be involved in their guidance or problems.

You can take a much wider perspective on how to use money as your wealth is not tied into any one business where you have a vested interest.

At this stage, you are mostly looking at multiple advantages from flexibility, tax breaks, access to investments not open to the general public and you are usually the first to be made aware of potential opportunities long before most.

Your role now young Jedi is to become aware of which quarter you are in presently and start to plan out your map to becoming a master JEDI which involves getting to an investor phase sooner rather than later.

Following the leap model will have you do exactly that!

You will then be the master of money and money will no longer be the master of you!

> **TO SUM UP: The Key Takeaways from this chapter:**
>
> • Getting a job is no guarantee of financial security.
>
> • There is a 4 stage JEDI model that most people are completely in the dark about which is moving from "Job owner" to "Employer" to "Director" to "Investor".
>
> • Reaching "Investor" stage is when you are a master Jedi although it is possible to be in more than just one stage at any one time

CHAPTER 41:
Why Must I Invest?

"Compound interest is the eighth wonder of the world. He who understands it earns it ... he who doesn't ... pays it. Compound interest is the most powerful force in the universe." – Albert Einstein

Investing and saving are quite different.

We need to start off with saving, but saving alone is too slow a process for you to get rich.

We need to invest as well!

The good news is that it is not difficult when you know how!

Investing is the process of learning how to make money work for you.

We have already given you some clues about how this works and have mentioned how assets are what put money in your pocket while liabilities take money out of your pocket.

Investing is all about finding assets that will build you more money from the money you have.

There is one specific tactic that can make investing the most powerful thing that you could ever do with your money.

We touched on this in Chapter 27 here in *I Need Money* and we did say we would come back to it.

Well, we are coming back to it now!

Don't be put off by the name, this can change your financial situation once you understand it.

Compound Interest.

Compound interest is the interest that you receive on interest.

It only works when you reinvest your interest that you are making back in on top of your initial investment and leave it untouched without making any withdrawals.

It is so powerful that Albert Einstein called it the most important invention in all of human history.

Simple interest is the interest that you make on the initial principal sum of money only.

Let's say that you had $10,000 invested in a high interested savings account paying 7% interest over three years, each year the interest you receive is 7% of $10,000 which is equal to $700.

This adds up to $1,700 of interest built up over three years.

Now imagine this time we invest the same amount of money with the exact same interest but this time it is "compounded annually".

At the end of year one, your $10,000 just as before will earn $700 interest.

However, in year 2 the interest of 7% is now paid on the new total of $10,000 + $700 = $10,700

The interest on this is $749 in year 2. In year 3, you are now earning 7% interest on $11,449.

Year 1	Year 2	Year 3
$10,000	$10,700	$11,449
+ $700	+ $749	+ $801.43

In total, you have earned $2,250.43 in compound interest instead of just $2,100 with simple interest.

While this is only a difference of $250.43 in 3 years, the effect gets larger and larger with every year that passes.

Let us take a real example so you can really see the power of this.

If we take the example where Person A, Mary invests her $10,000 at 7% per year and takes out the interest made every year while Person B John also invests $10,000 at 7% per year but leaves it compound over time.

After 30 years, John's investment is more than triple what Mary's is!

Now that is exciting enough, but let's show you what happens when the numbers we start with are higher.

Let's say that Mary and John started with $100,000 and add an extra $10,000 per year to their accounts.

Mary, however, needed the money after 15 years, but John could let it compound for 30 years.

Look what happens to the graph after a few more years, it starts to take off upwards very quickly!

There are some key learnings here, save as early as possible, save regularly, let the interest compound and leave it alone for as long as you can so that you can live off the interest for the rest of your life!

If you start now as a teen, your numbers will be a lot higher too!

You could actually turn one dollar a day into a million dollars over time if you let it compound at 12% per year and did nothing else!

Here is a quick little trick to allow you to work out what interest rate you need and how long it will take to double your money.

The trick is called the rule of 72.

If you divide the number 72 by any % interest rate, it lets you know approximately how many years it will take you to double your money.

Let's take an example. Let's say you want to know how long it will take to double your money when you save it at 7%.

The rule of 72 = 72/ 7 = 10.2 years to double your money.

If you find a return of 12%, then it would take you 72/12 = Only 6 years to double your money.

Remember the more money you can add and save along the way will help you reduce the time to double your money even faster.

What do we do to get started right away?

Step 1: Open a savings account in a local bank or credit union

Step 2: Start saving today by moving your "invest" jar funds into this account every week.

Step 3: Reinvest all of your interest.

Step 4: Leave the money alone.

There are many investment strategies that we can share with you once you have the basics in place.

In fact, we hope to share these with you very soon, and if you make your way over to funancialfreedom.com/investing we can show you how you can get started on your investing journey.

Investing strategies change over time and this is why it is important to keep you up to date on what the best investing strategies that you can implement at any particular time.

TO SUM UP: The Key Takeaways from this chapter:

- Compound interest is the most powerful force in the universe.

- It is the interest you receive on the interest.

- It only works if you leave it alone and if you do you can live on it for the rest of your life!

CHAPTER 42:
ACCELERATE – Wrapping Up

We have said a million times, the key to any success is keeping it simple.

Saving and Investing does not have to be complicated.

If it's complicated, you are not going to stick with it.

That's what we have created for you our simple Give/Save/Invest/Spend System.

10%/20%/20%/50%.

Simple!

However, most people have no system!

But most people are broke.

These are the headlines.

1 in 3 Americans have less than $5000 saved.

78% of Americans say they are 'extremely' concerned about not having enough money for retirement.

A shocking 21% of Americans have NOTHING saved for the future.

Some people, however, are more prepared.

And that's because the Rich, have good habits.

The Rich Give, Save and Invest.

And now you have the knowledge of how to do the same.

But remember what we said at the very beginning of this book?

Just having this knowledge means nothing.

Knowledge alone is worthless.

It only becomes valuable when you take action.

Knowledge without execution is poverty.

The secret to getting ahead - is getting started.

Otherwise, all this information that we are sharing with you, if you do nothing with it, you will remain in poverty.

SECTION 7: PLAY

www.funancialfreedom.com

CHAPTER 43:
PLAY – Introduction

"*Live the Life of Your Dreams: Be brave enough to live the life of your dreams according to your vision and purpose instead of the expectations and opinions of others.*" – Roy T. Bennett

The fourth and final step of the LEAP system is all about PLAY!!!

If we are going to work smart to Learn and Earn and Accelerate our money, there needs to be some reward at the end for us to look forward to ☺.

In this section, we are going to explore this.

Because we want you to live the best life you can possibly have.

But to do this – we have to grab life with both hands and get involved!

Life is a game.

We can choose to jump in and play, or stand on the sidelines and let it pass us by...

But nobody gets better at anything by standing on the sidelines.

The only way to get better at anything is to get involved.

So let's explore how you can play the game of life, and win!

CHAPTER 44:
Playing the Game of Life

Let us ask you a question.

Have you ever wondered why you find some things easy and fun while other things are a real drag?

Have you noticed that there are somethings that you will jump out of bed to get started on, but there are other things that you will find any excuse to avoid?

Interestingly, there is a reason for your behaviour.

It's all to do with what is known as your VALUES.

Learning how to win at the game of life starts with knowing your values.

But what does this even mean?

To put it simply, your values are the areas in your life that are most important to you.

So what's important to you?

Maybe it's spending time with your friends?

Maybe it's your physical appearance?

Maybe it's learning an instrument?

What do you not value as much?

Maybe it's studying and getting your homework done?

Think about the things in life that you need no encouragement to do – and the things in life that you find an effort to commit to.

What you like, and what you don't like, is linked to your Values.

However - the vast majority of society does not know what their values are.

In this chapter, we are going to identify what your values are.

Having this knowledge will significantly impact your physical and mental wellbeing.

Knowing your values and living to your highest values will result with you winning at the game of life!

REMEMBER THIS .... the key to living a happy fulfilled life is knowing what your values are and then learning how to fulfil them.

In fact – it's generally considered that there are eight different areas that our life can be broken up into.

And each one of these eight we will place a different value on as we proceed through life.

So let's take a look at what these eight are:

1: Physical:

This is attention to your physical body, your fitness, your interest in your appearance, your weight, your clothing, your exercise routines, your eating habits and anything at all related to how you look and feel.

If you value the 'physical', you will likely also find interesting the underlying physical systems that control your appearance and how it all works.

2: Financial:

The main focus here is money – cold, hard cash; how to earn it, save it, grow it, invest it, compound it and use it effectively.

This also means having a good understanding of the systems related to finances, such as the economy, trading, stock markets, choosing good companies to invest in, indexes, cryptocurrencies, foreign exchange currencies and basically anything related to growing money.

3: Spiritual:

Maybe this is one of your highest values – your spiritual wellbeing.

This can mean different things to different people.

In many cases, spiritual is associated with aligning to particular religious beliefs or dedicating one's life to a specific religious group.

This doesn't necessarily have to be the case, but traditionally it has been intertwined with different types of religious groups.

Your connection to a higher being or source is a significant priority.

More often this happens later in life.

4: Social:

If this is one of your higher values, this means your focus is on your impact socially.

Ranging from your immediate group of friends to your network of business relationships and, on a bigger scale, the influence you may have on a global social movement, perhaps on people's rights or for a cause that focuses on improving specific social issues.

For teens, social is usually the #1 value especially hanging with your peeps.

5: Mental:

If dedicating as much time as possible to learning something specific is important to you, then you have a high Mental Value.

Mental is associated with knowledge and educating yourself in a particular field of your choosing.

6: Vocational:

In this area, your vocation or career is your highest priority.

Many associate this directly with their place of work, their career or business, but this doesn't necessarily have to be the case.

Your vocation is your overall calling, and what you dedicate yourself to.

7: Familial:

This is one of the easiest areas to understand and one of the most popular of all areas, the focus being on your family.

This begins with your immediate family unit of parents and children and extended family.

It may go beyond this too, but the primary focus is on the people closest to you and your relationships with them.

8: Fun:

In this area, the name gives it away more than just a little.

It's where your main priority is fun, fun, fun.

Most of us as children grew up with fun being our highest value at all times and we'd love to keep it this way through life, but usually, that stops when the lack of money changes the rules of the game.

So, these are the eight areas of life, and every person has a different perspective on the world relating to their prioritisation of each of these areas.

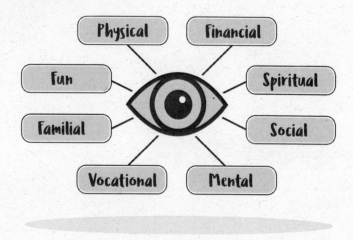

Fig 44.1: The eight areas of life

Now that you are aware of these different areas in life, we want to figure out what area is a priority in your life and we do this by working through your values.

How do you work out your values?

Can you change your values?

These are great questions.

There are a series of questions you can ask yourself to work out your values.

I am going to limit the questions to five areas here; there are many more you can ask, but these five will be enough to get you on the right track for now.

So to discover which values are most important to you – ask yourself these following questions.

Question 1: What do I spend most of my time on?

In which area do I spend my time more than any other?

To help you with this, we have created a table for you below.

Bring awareness to a typical day and assign roughly how much time you spend in each of the eight areas.

Trends will appear very quickly.

Because you have no choice but to attend school, the best way to do this is to analyse what you spend your time at school doing when you have a choice to do rather than being forced to do it.

	Value	Most Time Per Day
1.		
2.		
3.		
4.		
5.		
6.		
7.		
8.		

Table 44.1: Tracking time spent

Just write them down – don't judge, there is no right or wrong answer.

As we go through the questions, your answers will become more evident.

Question 2: What do I like to speak about with other people?

What topics of conversation light you up and what topics completely shut you down?

Imagine you are at a party and you don't know anyone there.

You are completely bored and about to nod off, when suddenly the topic of conversation changes, and you light up and become an entirely new person.

You know what the topic is, write it down...

	Value	Conversation Topics
1.		
2.		
3.		
4.		
5.		
6.		
7.		
8.		

Table 44.2: Tracking top areas of discussion

Question 3: What do I surround myself with at my place of study/work?

This is a very telling one, and it usually results in a few giggles.

People can immediately think of a friend who fits this acid test perfectly.

What images do you have on your lockers?

What images are on your screensavers?

All of these signs are very telling.

When you get older and potentially have a job where you work in an office or have visited your parents at work, you will start to notice that people in their offices have lots of pictures around them.

Usually, they do this to remind themselves why they spend their days and time doing things that they don't particularly enjoy doing or in some cases hate doing!

	Value	Images I Surround Myself With
1.		
2.		
3.		
4.		
5.		
6.		
7.		
8.		

Table 44.3: Tracking pictures in proximity

Question 4: How do I introduce myself to other people?

Self-labelling can be a great way of beginning to understand what your values are.

When you meet somebody new after you tell them your name, how do you next identify yourself?

"Hi, my name is POM, and I'm an athlete" or "I am a belieber!" or "I love the Golden State Warriors".

Each one will give a different indicator of what value may be your highest.

	Value	How I Introduce Myself
1.		
2.		
3.		
4.		
5.		
6.		
7.		
8.		

Table 44.4: Tracking self-appointed labels

You can also include as part of this, what do you wear on a regular basis?

You can often quite easily spot people who are more polarised in their values (focused much more on one than any of the others) because they spend significantly more time on one particular value, just by being aware of their physical appearance.

For example, if a gentleman enters a room and needs to turn sideways to get his muscular frame in the door, it is evident that he puts a lot of time in at the gym and is committed to his physical appearance.

Perhaps you may know someone who has long hair and wears a particular type of jewellery, and they almost float around.

This person might identify themselves as being quite spiritual and introduce themselves as "I AM..." followed by no label at all ☺.

Alternatively, the person always found in a suit and tie, even on a Sunday, is creating an impression that business or vocation is vital to them.

Or the "goth" image is quite distinct which is making it clear to others what you may or not believe in.

Once again there is no judgement here, in case you find that you are reacting negatively to any of the above. Yes, I agree 100% they are stereotypes, but I am purposely using examples that are polarised to get the point across.

Question 5: How do I spend my M"ONE"Y? What is MY ONE?

We have left what we've found to be the most valuable question of all to last.

It is possible to fudge the answers in the first 4, but this "ONE" is the true test to find out "M___Y" top values.

What you can do is to pull out your bank statements if you have them, or anywhere you track how you spend your money, from the last 3 months and go through each item one by one, putting a letter beside each item to identify which area you spent the money on.

Physical (P) Financial (F) Spiritual (S), Social (So), Mental (M), Vocational (V), Familial (Fa) and Fun (Fu).

This is a phenomenally powerful exercise, as it truly gives an insight into your daily behaviours, which add up to demonstrate the values that you live out in your life.

You will always spend your money in line with your values.

	Value	Most Money Spent
1.		
2.		
3.		
4.		
5.		
6.		
7.		
8.		

Table 44.5: Tracking spending of money

Imagine for a moment you are hanging out with your friend at their house.

You were just watching an advert on TV that was promoting an audio and video training set on financial mindset and investing strategies, and the product was $50.

Your friend immediately says, "Oh no, I can't afford that, in fact, there is no way I could afford that".

You suggest that you are interested, and you get the response "Are you crazy? Are you seriously considering this, spending $50 to learn how to grow your money? You've no money to learn to invest with!"

Finance is clearly not the highest of your friend's values, which is totally normal!

Naturally, they are looking to influence you based on their value systems.

Five minutes later, you are in a mall with your friend and they literally "find" $50 to purchase some clothing that was on sale as an "investment".

Either way, it is the same money, but in one case it was deemed affordable and in the other not.

It all depends on your individual values.

Where your money goes, focus and time soon flow!

Let's now pull together the results from part one of your values assessment in the key eight areas.

Take a look at each of the results in the tables 44.1 to 44.5 and collate them 1 to 8 based on which areas is most dominant to least prominent. Whichever appears as number "1" the most often becomes value #1 while the one that appears lowest overall gets placed as #8 and so on.

	Value	Overall Results
1.		
2.		
3.		
4.		
5.		
6.		
7.		
8.		

Table 44.6: Results of 8 areas review

When you complete this exercise, you will be able to determine rightly or wrongly how you spend your time and consequently your money based on your priority of values.

Other areas that you can explore are what you think about the most, what you are grateful for, what areas you are most organised in and where you put most of your energy?

As you get older, you will find that your spending patterns will become quite different from how they are at this moment in time.

Let's remind you, there is nothing inherently "right" or "wrong" with your values, they are yours.

However, with more awareness of the topic, more educated decisions can be made, and a situation that may be causing a lot of stress can begin to be adjusted, firstly by working on your values.

You need to ask yourself, do I want to have more money in my life and if so what do I need to do within my values to remedy this?

Now that you have gone through the five questions about your own values, you will have a much better appreciation of your personal priorities and spending behaviours and how you choose to allocate your time, thoughts, energy and space.

You will naturally find it easier to do things that are high in your values and shy away from the rest.

You can keep this in mind as you set your priorities in the next chapter when you start setting goals.

Every single person has a unique value system fingerprint; no two people's values are exactly the same.

If you look hard enough, you will find someone with exactly the opposite of your values, and more than likely you would not agree with this person on much!

At school, there will be some people you naturally are drawn to because subconsciously you can tell by their appearance that they may have similar values to your own.

The opposite is also true, where you immediately can dislike someone you haven't even spoken to because you anticipate that you have differing values.

As soon as you know what your values are, you can very quickly understand what inspires you.

You are naturally inspired to do those things that are high in your values.

It is the area in life where you have the most order, structure, no one needs to remind you about it, in fact, you will jump out of bed first thing in the morning to do it.

Time disappears when working on your highest values.

The word "inspiration" comes from the word to "inspire", or to breathe in.

You are inspired by what comes from within.

Motivation, on the other hand, is when you require an external force to get you to do something that is naturally low in your values.

If you need to be motivated to do something, it means you are attempting to live to someone else's values and not yours.

Ahem... does this remind you of your parents or teachers "motivating" you?

They are the external force pushing you against your current value set.

They, of course, have their values and they have ideas for what you should be doing according to their values!

This is why you need "motivation" from parents and teachers to get you to do the things you really don't want to do!

This can never last in the long term but is required in many cases to pass exams.

Your parents and teachers obviously want the best for you too so often it is best to at least listen to what they are asking for you to do as they do have more experience on the planet and remember one day you may be speaking to your children!

> **TO SUM UP: The Key Takeaways from this chapter:**
>
> - Becoming aware of your value structure can mean the difference between a life of misery and a life of inspiration.
>
> - There are eight different areas that we can focus on to surmise what our values are at this point in life.
>
> - Your values change as you move through life.
>
> - How you spend your money is a major indicator of what you value the most.

CHAPTER 45:
Your Dream Life

"If you aim at nothing, you will hit every time." – Zig Ziglar

We have taken a considerable step forward in that last chapter and uncovered your values.

Make sure, if you haven't already, to take some time out and do the exercise as you have to work out what is most important to you.

Once we know our values, the next step is to look into the future and look at your "future self".

What would your ideal future self be doing?

What would a perfect day look like?

What would you love to be, do and have?

What country would you be living in?

What would you do with your day if your lack of money was not an issue?

You can fill in what your perfect life would look like below. Have fun – there is no right and wrong here.

Your Dream Life

Fig 45.1: Your Dream Life

You can download and print out a copy of this at
funancialfreedom.com/resources.

Allow approximately 20 or 30 minutes to fill in your Dream Life.

Just keep writing solidly about what you want, what you would love to have, what you'd love to be, where you'd love to go, etc.

It might take a bit of time to get into the flow but when you do you might find you get a little greedy and you start writing down all kinds of things.

We recommend you include all eight areas of life that we went through: physical, financial, spiritual, social, mental, familial, vocational and fun. If you're into sports, you could include in your dream life that you will go to the Super Bowl, or the Olympics, or the World Cup. Maybe you'd like to scuba dive or go paragliding or parachuting.

If you're into travel, you could add to your Dream Life that you'd like to see the Great Barrier Reef, or the Pyramids, or the Northern Lights.

Whatever it is for you, be sure to write it down, big dreams and little dreams.

Keep writing regardless of how unbelievable what you are writing may seem.

Be imaginative.

Be creative.

Don't limit yourself.

It doesn't need to be just for you, you can do it for your family or friends as well.

Do it for whoever and whatever really drives you and inspires you.

When you're writing, it's a good idea to write it in the present tense, as if you already have it.

Don't stop until you feel you have left nothing out.

If you're still writing, and 45 minutes has elapsed, that's great, just keep going.

There's no need to stop because the more you get, the more powerful this exercise is.

Now one important thing to remember is that no one else is going to see this but you.

You won't be sharing this with anybody unless someone who you know will really support you.

Sometimes if you share this with the wrong person, they might think that you're a bit crazy, or they can knock you back without intending to, more so because they're just scared actually of the possibility that you could achieve this dream life and they may not be in your future plans.

The difference between a dream and goal is that one doesn't have a plan and the other does.

We will start with your dreams and then make them goals ☺

Get writing, make it real and suddenly you will become very protective of your time!

Write on as many pieces of paper as you need!

The next stage after writing out your hopes and dreams is to start to put some realistic timelines around them and turn them into goals.

The first thing that we'd like you to do is to actually take what you have written down as your wish list, and start to organise them into specific one-sentence goals.

If you have written something like, "I'm in the Bahamas, and I'm having a fantastic time" in your dream life, you can modify this to something like, "I am visiting the Bahamas by the 15th of March, 2028, or earlier, where I'll spend two weeks on a cruise."

The writing of goals in a specific format is critical. There are lots of theories around this, but mostly the tried and tested S.M.A.R.T. goals.

We prefer to use a more advanced version of this called S.M.A.R.T.E.R. goals ☺!

Firstly it must be in the present tense, using the language of "I am" rather than "I will be".

Then we can start the SMARTER acronym to lead us the rest of the way.

The letters as you can see may have different variations of the word, but all generally mean the same thing.

S.pecific (simple, sensible, significant)

M.easurable (meaningful, motivating)

A.chievable (agreed, attainable)

R.elevant (reasonable, realistic and resourced, results-based)

T.imebound (time-based, time limited, time/cost limited, timely, time-sensitive)

E.valuated (expectations, enriches values and estimated)

R.eviewed (reasonable and researched)

Specific:

The more specific the goal, the more real it becomes and the more you can genuinely believe in it and have it inspiring to you.

Here are some questions to consider;

What is it exactly?

Why do I want it?

Where will it happen?

Who else is involved and benefiting from this?

What resources might I need?

In other words, something like "being happy" isn't going to cut it!

Measurable:

There must be a method of knowing how you will measure and track performance on the way towards the outcome.

This can help you to maintain motivation along the journey, track results as you go and most importantly react early enough and seek assistance if you veer off track and need help to get back on target.

Here are some questions to consider; how much, how many, how will I know I am on or off track?

Achievable:

Your goal needs to be realistic and attainable for you to feel that this is within your grasp with the right focus and support.

There is a dilemma of what is considered attainable for most people!

If you set the bar too low then it's not inspiring, but if you set the goal too high, you can lose motivation as you can very quickly see that you are way off track.

What we have found, is that you generally tend to be overly optimistic in the areas that you are not really empowered in which for me were business and money.

Questions to consider are: do I feel this goal is attainable by myself?

What about with focus and support from the right people?

Who can I ask with experience in this area to see if this is attainable?

Relevant:

Having spent the time on clarifying your values and what areas are important to you at this point in your life, choosing goals that are relevant to your values will be a lot easier than it may have been in the past.

If you don't have a value on it, why would you ever do it!

Questions to ask yourself are: is this goal in line with my higher values?

Can I see how this serves me?

Can I see how this goal takes me to heaven?

Timebound:

No goal is complete by having an "end date", the date by which the task will be accomplished.

For now, you can choose the time frame that you feel is realistic.

When writing it down, be sure to add "or sooner" to allow yourself to finish well ahead of the deadline if progress is made even quicker than you expect.

The actual time that you may finish up with on each goal may change after we evaluate goals and work out what is realistic in the overall framework of planning.

Evaluated:

A major downside of the traditional SMART goal setting techniques is the lack of quantification of what is realistic or not. Assessing whether this goal is in-line with and enriches your values is important to ensure we are aligned with our overall expectations and dreams.

Reviewed:

No goal is truly complete until we implement a review system to keep track of progress. Some questions to ask are: What are the indicators that I can use to measure progress? Do I have a system in place to review my goals at least on a weekly basis? With these measures in place, are these goals reasonable?

Let's take an example of a financial goal:

I am earning $1,000 or more per month (after tax) from the sales of my physical and audio books by 20 July 2022.

Let's take an example of a health goal:

I am exercising daily for a minimum of 15 minutes and have a resting heart rate of 50 bpm and body fat of 10% by 20 July 2025.

As you can see they do not need to be very long.

Dreams to Reality		
What	When	Area

Table 45.1: Dreams to Reality

You can download and print out a copy of this at funancialfreedom.com/resources.

Start working your way through your dream day and start to turn your generalisations into specifics and in the column on the right-hand side for "When", put in a time that you would like to have this achieved by.

Each line should now be written in the SMARTER format.

Put in when you think that's achievable, ten years, five years, six months, whatever it is.

Every goal will be slightly different, and there doesn't need to be any organisation to the sequence.

You are turning your longer essay in fig 45.1 "Your Dream Life" into line-by-line goals that you want to achieve so, please put in the "when" associated with each item.

Don't worry about having your "when" in both on the goal and in the "when" column, this just allows us to quickly see where you are over committing so we can go back and make edits on time expectations a little later.

 The next step is to place the first initial in the final column that says "area" for what the goal is.

What area in life is that goal for you?

For example, for financial, you can use "F," physical health "P," spiritual "S," vocational "V," family "F," contribution and social "C," mental "M," and fun just a smiley face.

We strongly suggest you do it for all the areas even though you will have a natural tendency to focus on those that are your higher values.

So for example, let's say it was about health. You can write, "I am a size two by 11/5/2023", then you put in by when, 11/5/2023 in the "when" column.

In the "area" column, you would put in "P" for physical health.

Then the next one could be, "I am earning $5000 a month or more after tax from my main job by 2/5/2026."

Then you put in the specific "when", whatever you feel is reasonable for you with your current best guess, whether it's 6 months or 36 months, and in "area", it would be "F" for finance.

Now this will all come together, and you'll see why you're doing this very shortly.

The next part of the workbook is about your vision of your future you in each individual area.

Once you have organised your goals by area, where you have all the different letters in the column, you can then look at the goals that you have in each area, and start to group them together.

Whatever you have for physical, put all of them together.

Whatever you have for finance, put all them together and so on.

This is to allow you to create a vision of future self of what you'd like to see in each area of your life.

For each area of your life, you now have written goals, and you'll probably start to see a picture of a clear theme or direction of what you truly want, as opposed to the all too common feeling of uncertainty.

Once organised by area, you can then start to look at the goals that you have in each area for trends to see what the common themes are.

My Vision
Financial:
Vocational:
Physical Health:
Spiritual Matters:
Social / Contribution:
Familial:
Mental / Growth:
Fun:

Table 45.2: Your Vision of your Future Self in Key eight Areas

This vision document will give you a much clearer picture of where you actually see your life going, and why you're setting these goals in the first place is because you want to achieve this overall vision.

Your vision in each area may change in time.

The point is you need to start now and get this down on paper so that you can look at it maybe in a couple of years and laugh, or you could look at it and go, "Wow, I've really got very close, or I'm on the way to achieving what I have in my vision."

With tables 45.1 and 45.2 completed, now it is time to put more long-term thinking around this.

We can take each of the goals and put them into a template planning out what those goals would look like over a 10 to 15 year period.

We can also set shorter term goals based on the things we would need to achieve in order to reach our 10 to 15 year goals.

Goals	6 months	1 year	2 – 3 years	4 – 6 years	7 – 10 years	10 – 15 years
Financial:						
Vocational/ Business:						
Physical Health:						
Spiritual Matters:						
Social:						
Mental / Growth:						
Familial:						
Fun:						

Table 45.3: Your 10-15 Year Goals

Remember you have a soft copy print version of this that you can type into if you wish at funancialfreedom.com/resources.

In the first column, you should see that I have the different areas for which you are setting your goals.

They are organised in the sequence financial, then your business and vocational, physical health, spiritual matters, relationships, mental growth, familial and fun. To speed up the process, start with the areas that come more naturally to you to get into an inspired flow.

Each of the columns on the right-hand side is timelines from 6 months up to 10 – 15 years.

You may notice that from year 2 onwards, we have grouped timelines spanning over a few years for example 2-3 years, 4-6 years, 7-10 years and 10 -15 years.

The reason being it is tough having not done this exercise before and being unaware of your future capabilities to predict too specifically when you will be complete.

This method allows you to become more specific over time as you move towards that goal.

What we recommend you do is to start on the far right-hand side and think about where you want to be in 10 to 15 years' time.

In this table, there is only room for three different goals for each, and that is more than enough for now!

This forward-thinking process allows you to start to then work backwards from your future and think, "Okay, if that's where I want to be in 10 years, well, where do I need to be in 8 years?

Where do I need to be in 5 years, 3 years, this year, six months' time?"

What's my first step today?

Make your 10 to 15 year targets both motivational and inspirational for you.

There's no point in having a target in here that isn't going to drive you forward, then it is not truly a goal ready for this list.

The whole point of having the goal here in 15 years' time is that you think, "Do you know what? I'm really motivated to do this.

I'm really inspired to do this, and I'm actually going to do what I need to do to achieve this."

Let's have a check in at this point! How are you feeling?

There are any number of possibilities, the first being "fine", I haven't been doing any of the actions ... LOL!

Ok, please stop now and get to work!

A lot is going on here, 8 areas, 3 goals each, across 6 different time brackets!

Maybe you are feeling a little overwhelmed with the amount of work just outlined, and you have started it but are a bit stuck.

This is very common, all you need to do is go back and quickly recap what you have done, follow along with the book and then proceed through the next section.

A very common response for people when starting the 15-year goals exercise is "I don't know what I want".

Most adults have no clue where they would like to be in 5 years, let alone 15 years.

That is why we want to share this with you so early in life so that you get the bigger picture sooner and understand why being financially smart as such an important role to play in making these dreams a reality.

Perhaps you feel really good, amazing in fact!

We're guessing you have taken the time to complete the exercise and you are really starting to feel that you are getting some shape around who you are, what you want to achieve and its inspiring to you!

Fantastic!

That is precisely how it should feel!

There is an excellent quote from Selk, Bartow and Ruddy, "Greatness is predicated on consistently doing things others can't or won't do".

Doing what we ask you to do next is one of those tasks that fall into that category, and this is creating a physical, printed goal card.

It is the Top Goal in each of the 8 areas that you now take and type out into your "Balanced Goal Card", which you can laminate and carry with you at all times. You choose the goals and make sure it is written as previously stated and set it for 15 years from now.

This is the template that we use, and you can download your own version from funancialfreedom.com/resources.

Figure 45.2: Balanced Goal Card

Now you will have your big 8 on your person at all times.

Remember, you can at any time look at those goals and ask the question, "What is the ONE thing that I am going to do today to get closer to achieving this goal?" and you will be well on the way to a new life.

TO SUM UP: The Key Takeaways from this chapter:

- Identifying what your dream life would look like allows you to set goals to allow you to make this dream a reality.

- Taking general statements and making them specific allows you to set plans to achieve your goals.

- Printing and carrying your goals with you has a very powerful impact on the success rate of achieving your goals.

CHAPTER 46:
Your Vision Board

"The most pathetic person in the world is someone who has sight but no vision." – Helen Keller

The best way to get started with PLAY in your life is taking the goals you have just set and surrounding yourself with imagery that inspires you around those specific goals.

Something to look at each morning and every night that makes you feel amazing when you look at it.

You may have come across this idea before; it is called a VISION board.

It is a really FUN thing to do no matter how naff it might feel, to begin with.

You can start off by thinking about different areas in life that might be important to you now relating to FUN, Health, Financial, Social, Vocational and Family.

Go to google.com/images and look for images that really inspire you about all the cool things you could be doing… maybe surfing or snowboarding.

Think about the places you could be visiting. More to come on this shortly.

Imagine the body you want to have.

Think about the girlfriend/boyfriend of your dreams.

What does your dream car look like?

What about a boat?

What is your dream house looking like?

You can look at this example and start to use it as a possible template.

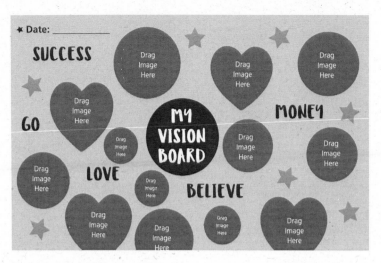

Fig 46.1: Your Vision Board

Let your imagination run riot, have no boundaries, just go for it!

Once you have it complete, put it somewhere in your bedroom where you see it every day and night.

Take a picture with your phone, and you can use it as a screensaver to remind you why you are doing what you are doing with the LEAP model.

In the next few chapters, we will look at four specific areas as part of "PLAY" that hopefully made it onto your vision board in some form or another:

- Inspiring Trips

- Being Healthy

- Making a difference

- Competition time

TO SUM UP: The Key Takeaways from this chapter:

- Play means different things to different people.

- Play is not only about what you can buy but who you can help, and the difference you can make to others.

- A vision board will help you feel inspired to really go after your goals!

CHAPTER 47:
Inspiring Trips...

Most people find nothing more enjoyable than visiting a brand new country with brand new people and experiences.

But did you know, less than 40% of all US citizens have passports!

That means only 4 in 10 Americans are able to leave the US to visit places such as Europe, Australia and anywhere else in-between.

Which is a shame because travel expands your mind and expands your soul.

And above all - it's FUN!

Many people use travel to inspire them.

Think of your home as the world, and every country a different room.

So, with that in mind, in this Chapter, we wanted to get your creative juices flowing as to some of the incredible places in the world that you can visit.

Let's start with some of the most inspiring trips that have been voted best in the world for teens

Firstly — European City Breaks.

Just a few days in a new city can be a hugely rewarding experience and a very cool thing to do.

From the cafe culture of Amsterdam to the unique character of Barcelona.

From the historically enchanting city of Rome to the magic and romance of Paris.

There are many fantastic cities that you should put on your wish list.

But let us whet your appetite by sharing with you the top 5 most popular cities to visit in Europe.

Paris – The City of Light

The capital of France and one of the most beautiful cities in the world.

It has stunning architecture, fantastic food, and some of the most fashionable shops, art, museums and history.

And then there's Barcelona.

A jewel of tourism in Europe. Barcelona in Spain boasts culture, sport, shopping and nightlife. It's a city famous for never sleeping.

Rome is completely unique.

Famous for the heritage of the Colosseum, the Forum, and the Vatican, Rome draws crowds all year round to experience its wealth of ancient history and beauty.

Staying with Italy, Venice has to be seen to be experienced. Set in a lagoon in North Eastern Italy, Venice is made up of 177 canals, 400 bridges and 118 islands packed full of history, art and charm.

Or how about London?

In fact, London is many people's number 1 city to visit.

It's often been voted the world's capital city for short breaks.

And it is one of the most amazing cities in the World.

London has almost an endless collection of historical and modern sites all in one place – Buckingham Palace, the Houses of Parliament, the Tower of London, St Paul's Cathedral, the Shard and the London Eye to name just a few.

And if you factor in parks galore, river trips and lots for the entire family to get involved with - you have one of the most rounded cities to visit.

Aside from Europe, of course, there are many other world cities that you should consider to add to your to-do list.

But top of that list has to be New York.

Everybody should experience New York City at least once in their life.

It's a feast for anyone, of any age.

But as a teen, you will be spoiled for choice.

New York City wears many crowns.

You can experience the glitz and glamour of some of the most iconic landmarks in the world.

It's the dining and shopping capital of the world.

From Broadway to Brooklyn, from Times Square to the Empire State, NYC is an irresistible feast for all.

A few things you should consider doing when visiting NYC include:

Visiting the Statue of Liberty.

Take the Staten Island Ferry at night to experience the magnificence of the Manhattan Skyline.

Walk or bike or row or ice skate in Central Park.

Take a Double Decker City Bus Tour.

Moving further afield - another dazzling city you should add to your to-do list is Cape Town.

It's nestled by the breathtaking Table Mountain and has beautiful scenery just waiting to be explored.

Hong Kong is for many the ultimate city break destination.

Sample traditional cuisine, marvel at towering skyscrapers and hike some seriously awesome trails, all in one place.

Better yet, relax after a day of sightseeing in one of their excellent hotels.

And staying with cities, how about Dubai? It has a whole host of exciting theme parks, the largest shopping mall on Earth and some of the best beaches in the world.

All we are wanting to do here - is explore some ideas of places you can visit to allow you to PLAY.

If you're a surf fan, how about a surf holiday?

Hawaii, Tahiti, Bali and Mexico all are home to some of the world's best-surfing sites.

Dual Destination vacations are a great way to have a jam-packed trip, full of different experiences.

Have you considered one of these? You could spend the first few days enjoying a beach vacation, before swapping for something completely different, maybe a jungle hike, or a safari, for the remainder of your trip.

It's a big, beautiful world and there is a lot to see. A Dual Destination Vacation allows you to see more than one place in a single trip.

Maybe experiencing nature in the raw, is something that makes you feel alive.

In that case - where do we start?

From the volcanoes and Northern Lights of Iceland - to the dusty Colorado river hikes along Grand Canyon - to the spectacular natural beauty of Machu Picchu.

Experiencing even just a few days in some of the world's greatest adventure playgrounds is enough to make you feel completely energized and ready to take on more in life.

TO SUM UP: The Key Takeaways from this chapter:

- A great way to play is to travel

- Travel broadens the mind and inspires you to do more, to be more and to see more.

- No matter where you live in the world there are places both near and far that can take your breath away

- Travel is so much better when you can enjoy it with friends and family!

CHAPTER 48:
Being Healthy

"Health is like money. We never have a true idea of its value until we lose it" – *Josh Billings*

You have probably heard your parents or grandparents tell you that your health is your wealth.

Well, that's sort of true!

It doesn't pay the bills though as you now know.

We do however want to be in fantastic condition and to be around for a long, long time to enjoy it.

The most amazing part of being alive today is that the technology now exists that will allow you to print identical organs to the ones you have!

In other words, when you get older, for the first time in human history, you will be able to look younger!

Imagine looking like a 20-year-old when you are 90!

Yes, the future is here, it's just not spread out evenly.

Those with the money will be able to look more amazing the older they get.

How incredible is that, as most people growing old and wrinkly and forgetful while this is all going to be something of the past very soon with 3D printing technology and gene therapy.

But for now, rather than booking ourselves into surgery for new hair and hearts, let's look at what we can do in the short term

"You are what you eat."

If you eat rubbish, you feel like rubbish.

The earlier you start into clean living habits which are actually really easy to add into your life, the better it is for your health, and the longer you can live.

Simple things like always sipping water all day long.

Adding slices of lime to your water and taking green capsules will keep your body alkaline and fight off diseases.

Eating an 80% water based diet like salads, fruit and vegetables would be awesome!

Playing sports especially those that involve teamwork not only are fun, but great for health and meeting that person of your dreams ...who knows!!

Start the habit of health early so that you can have a very wealthy and healthy future.

Just like money compounds, so to do the effects of continuous health habits and avoiding health withdrawals like toxins as much as you possibly can!

> **TO SUM UP: The Key Takeaways from this chapter:**
>
> - You only know the value of your health when you lose it.
>
> - We are living in amazing times where growing older no longer means getting old.
>
> - Simple, easy to adapt health habits can have a huge difference in the long run.

CHAPTER 49:
Making a Difference

One of the most rewarding things you can do in your life is to you use your money and influence to help those less well off than you.

If you look at the wealthiest people on the planet, most of them have this in common, they put their money into good causes.

Philanthropy is the desire to promote the welfare and wellbeing of others, especially by the generous donation of money to good causes.

The interesting thing is that the more wealthy people become, the more they want to make a positive difference on the planet!

How inspiring is that?

We are often told that rich people are mean people or that you can't get to the top unless you trample over everyone else to get there, but this is far from the truth in most cases.

In today's world, the wealthiest people lead by example for the rest of us.

One of the main aims of FUNancial Freedom, the company behind this book, is to encourage all of our students to help other teens that live in less well-off areas in the world to apply the same tactics that you now know.

As part of your support of this book, you are allowing us to help thousands of students all over the world in places like India, Nepal, China, Latin America, South Africa, Kenya, Ethiopia, Somalia, and many more to become empowered when it comes to their money.

We would love to invite you on this journey with us, and you can find out more here at http://funancialfreedom.com/resources.

You may also have your own personal causes that you wish to support with your money, maybe to do with animals, or the homeless, of the curing of particular diseases.

There is no shortage of causes.

It would be absolutely fantastic if you could look to set up your own foundation to support your own cause.

A foundation is a "legal category of nonprofit organization that will typically either donate funds and support to other organizations or provide the source of funding for its own charitable purposes."

This is a fancy way of saying that it is a company that helps others but the profits go to the cause once the costs of running the business have been covered.

By donating to charity, there is no guarantee that the money donated goes to where you expect it to go.

With your own foundation, you can decide where the money goes.

It also allows you to leave a "legacy", something that will outlive you and inspire others all over the world and will enable you to have a global impact!

TO SUM UP: The Key Takeaways from this chapter:

- Philanthropy is the desire to promote the welfare and well-being of others, expressed especially by the generous donation of money to good causes.

- Creating a foundation can allow someone to make a global impact and leave a long-term legacy long after their life.

- FUNancial Freedom are assisting young teens all over the world in many developing countries to learn the skills to empower themselves around wealth.

CHAPTER 50:
Competition

There is nothing like a little bit of healthy competition to make life interesting. I'm sure you'll agree!

What if you were not undertaking the tasks in this goal alone, or even just with your friends?

What if we could set you up to enter a friendly competition with students just like you all over the world?

How cool would that be right?

Well, it's happening...

When it comes to health, one of the measures used to define how healthy somebody is at any particular point in time is the BMI index.

The BMI index stands for Body Mass Index and is a measure of body fat based on height and weight that applies to adult men and women.

We are going to measure the health of your wealth too using the same scoring method, with BMI!

At FUNancial Freedom, our BMI stands for:

• Business

• Money

• Impact

We are going to calculate how well you are adapting what you learned in the LEARN section and then applied in the EARN section to create your business or businesses.

We will assign a measure of your score in Business based on the profitability of the business.

We will have to rely on your honesty here as we can not check all of your numbers!

In the Money part, we will look at the savings and investment plans that you have in place based on the learnings in the ACCELERATE section.

We will assign scores based on what you have in place and how much you have compounded and how well the money is being managed.

We will outline criteria for you so you will know exactly how to do this.

Finally, the "I" is for impact.

This is where you have the opportunity to get the most points.

It is the impact that you are having on others both at home and abroad.

You could use the word "inspiration" just as quickly as we want to measure that you can leave a meaningful contribution too.

We want you to take these learnings and use them to produce an impact that truly makes a difference on this planet.

Please feel free to send us in your inspirational stories so we can share them with others to positively impact on them too!

This is all available to join on our FUNancial app which you can download from the android or apple store on your smartphone very soon.

TO SUM UP: The Key Takeaways from this chapter:

- Competition is a great way to encourage people to take more focused action.

- Your success in "*I Need Money*" will be measured in three areas, your "BMI" index, or Business, Money and Impact.

- Making a contribution beyond yourself and especially to the less fortunate financially is one of our primary aims.

CHAPTER 51:
PLAY – Wrapping Up

So, that's it for PLAY.

Remember - the whole purpose of *I Need Money* is to break down the 4 steps - to making, investing and growing your money.

And we do this by using our LEAP method.

Learn. Earn. Accelerate. Play.

Each one of the 4 steps are important.

It's been proven time and time again - that having a goal to aspire to - something that you can picture in your mind's eye is often the difference between success and failure.

That's why having a strong vision of something to do that is FUN - is vital.

So, our advice would be - go through the exercises we have laid out for you here in PLAY.

Write down your values - write down your goals.

Write down what you would like your ideal life to look like.

And then, get specific about what PLAY is for you.

The reason many people fail in life is not because they aim too high and miss, but because they aim too low and hit.

So, don't settle for second best.

Write down what you want your life to be lived, and then follow the LEAP method to make it happen.

SECTION 8:
Conclusion

www.funancialfreedom.com

CHAPTER 52:
Next Steps

WOW....what a hell of a ride that was!

Firstly, CONGRATULATIONS!

You've made it ... you have reached the end of this book, but honestly, it is only the start of a most magnificent journey!

We made some pretty big claims at the start of this book, and we hope that not only do you now feel educated on the topic of money and feeling financially smarter but that you also are super PUMPED and EXCITED about the next stages of your money journey.

You are not alone here!

There are literally thousands of teens just like you all over the world starting off on this journey, and very soon it will be millions!

Together we are not only going to make a difference, but we are also going to be the difference!

Together we will be able to show anyone, no matter how bad their starting point is, no matter what the perceived disadvantage is, how to take control of My ONE .... MoneY ... and become financially smarter, financially more empowered and ultimately live happier more impactful lives!

Every single day, we can make someone else's life so much better with the knowledge you now have.

A book is still just a book, however.

Knowledge is not power, it is the application of the content in here that ultimately makes the difference between "shelf-development" and "self-development!"

Your journey starts now, and we wish to help you for an entire lifetime, not only while you are a teen.

You are just about finished with the *"I Need money"* book and the LEAP model for teens right now.

BUT, have you ever heard of a QUANTUM leap before?

A quantum leap is a term used in chemistry when something is a very significant and sudden increase in its size, amount, or quality.

A major leap to a new level.

Well, that is what we are after throughout your entire lifetime, one leap after the next allowing you to make massive increases in knowledge and income.

You won't know this, but *"I Need Money"* for teens is part of an overall lifelong plan for your money mastery.

There are 7 levels in the Q.U.A.N.T.U.M.

Q.uantify

U.nderstand

A.ccelerate

N.urture

T.en X

U.nify

M.agnify

These trainings are spread out over a lifetime starting with the age groups of 3-7, 8-11, 11-15, 15-19, 20+, 30+ and 40+.

Right now, you are in the accelerate stages where you are taking your basic knowledge from school and rapidly accelerating your learning with our help.

Your next stage is the Nurture stage where we take your learnings and understanding and start to bed in or nurture the development.

We need to ensure that we nurture the seedlings that you have now put in place.

You will need to learn how to grow your businesses to the next level.

You will need to take your savings and learn how to grow those investments and maximize the compound effect.

"We are either growing or dying" is a very well-known saying that is very true.

With money, it is no different, your knowledge of it is either being applied or wasted.

Your money is either growing or being spent.

We are going to make sure that through your journey in this life, that we will be your guides all the way if you will allow us!

It's time for a quantum leap, time for the next level!

And we are waiting for you to be your guides…

It's now time to take this journey to the next step and allow us to become a part of your daily life!

It's time to join us on your phone and tablet.

Every day we will send you quick tips to keep you focused, to keep your eyes on the prize!

Speaking of prizes, there will be lots of those too!

We can't wait to hear about your successes and the impact you are having.

Please let us help you every single day from now on with our brand new funanical app and by joining our membership program which is designed to keep you on track and propel you to brand new leaps!

If you want more money in your pocket, make sure that you carry us with you in your pocket every day, and we will be sure to help you earn, manage and grow more!

You are so nearly there!

Thank you so much for sharing this journey with us, and we cannot wait to get started on the next stage of this journey together!

Why wait? Let's get over there right now to funancialfreedom.com.

Scan with Facebook Messenger to get started. In the App, tap on your profile picture in the top right corner, tap your picture at the top of the page, tap Scan Code to scan.